A Practical Guide for Policy Analysis

A Practical Guide for Policy Analysis: The Eightfold Path to More Effective Problem Solving

Eugene Bardach

Richard and Rhoda Goldman School of Public Policy
University of California at Berkeley

CHATHAM HOUSE PUBLISHERS

SEVEN BRIDGES PRESS, LLC

NEW YORK • LONDON

Seven Bridges Press, LLC
135 Fifth Avenue
New York, NY 10010

Publisher: Robert J. Gormley
Managing Editor: Katharine Miller
Cover and Interior Design: Andrea Barash Design
Composition: Bytheway Publishing Services
Printing and Binding: Versa Press, Inc.

Library of Congress Cataloging-in-Publication Data

Bardach, Eugene.
   A practical guide for policy analysis : the eightfold path to more
effective problem solving / Eugene Bardach.
         p.   cm.
Includes bibliographical references.
   ISBN 1-889119-29-6
   1. Policy sciences. 2. Decision making. 3. Problem solving. I.
Title.
   H97.B37 2000
   320′.6—dc21   99-050621

Manufactured in the United States of America

10   9   8   7   6   5   4

Contents

Preface

THIS IS A HANDBOOK of concepts and methods for working your way through a policy analysis. The presumed user is a beginning practitioner preparing to undertake a policy analysis. I have developed the general approach and many of the specific suggestions over twenty-five years of teaching policy analysis workshops to first- and second-year graduate students at the Richard and Rhoda Goldman School of Public Policy, University of California, Berkeley. I have also found this handbook useful in teaching an undergraduate introduction to public policy and for executive education groups.

The handbook assumes a familiarity with basic economic concepts, including those having to do with market failures (including market imperfections). It is not meant to stand alone but should be used in conjunction with other sources. Five of the best textbooks in policy analysis, which amplify points in this handbook, are

- Edith Stokey and Richard Zeckhauser, *A Primer for Policy Analysis* (New York: Norton, 1978).
- David L. Weimer and Aidan R. Vining, *Policy Analysis: Concepts and Practice* (Upper Saddle River, N.J.: Prentice Hall, 1999).
- Robert D. Behn and James W. Vaupel, *Quick Analysis for Busy Decision-Makers* (New York: Basic Books, 1982).
- Lee S. Friedman, *Microeconomic Policy Analysis* (New York: McGraw-Hill, 1984)—revised edition forthcoming.
- Duncan MacRae Jr., and Dale Whittington, *Expert Advice for Policy Choice: Analysis and Discourse* (Washington, D.C.: Georgetown University Press, 1997).

I wish to acknowledge the patience of and the helpful reactions from all the students and friends who have made use of this handbook, especially those who put up with its earlier versions. Special thanks are due to Robert Behn, Sandford

Borins, Jose Canela-Cacho, Hank Dempsey, David Dery, John Ellwood, Lee Friedman, David Garcia-Junco Machado, Nina Goldman, David Kirp, Jake Lavin, Leo Levenson, Martin A. Levin, Duncan MacRae, Carolyn Marzke, John Mendeloff, Michael O'Hare, Steven Page, Eric Patashnik, Beryl Radin, Andres Roemer, Larry Rosenthal, Mark Sabean, Eugene Smolensky, David Weimer, and Marc Zegans.

Introduction

POLICY ANALYSIS is a social and political activity. True, you take personal moral and intellectual responsibility for the quality of your policy-analytic work. But policy analysis goes beyond personal decision making. First, the subject matter concerns the lives and well-being of large numbers of our fellow citizens. Second, the process and results of policy analysis usually involve other professionals and interested parties: it is often done in teams or officewide settings; the immediate consumer is a "client" of some sort like a hierarchical superior; and the ultimate audience will include diverse subgroups of politically attuned supporters and opponents of your work. All of these facts condition the nature of policy-analytic work and have a bearing on the nature of what is meant by *quality work*.

A policy analyst can work in any number of positions. Once upon a time, the term implied someone rather wonkish who worked in a large government bureaucracy serving up very technical projections of possible policy impacts for one or more policy alternatives to some undersecretary of planning. No longer. Policy analysts help in planning, budgeting, program evaluation, program design, program management, public relations, and other functions. They work alone, in teams, and in loose networks that cut across organizations. They work in the public, nonprofit, and for-profit spheres. Although their work is ideally distinguished by transparency of method and interpretation, the analysts themselves might explicitly bring to their jobs the values and passions of advocacy groups as well of "neutral" civil servants. The professional networks in which they work might contain—in most cases, do contain—professionals drawn from law, engineering, accounting, and so on, and in those settings the policy-analytic point of view has to struggle for the right to counter—or better yet, synthesize—the viewpoints of the other professionals. Although policy-analytic work products typically involve written reports, they may also include briefings, slide presentations, magazine articles, and TV interviews. The recipients of these products may be broad and diffuse audiences as well as narrowly construed paying clients or employers. The advice in this handbook is directed both to policy analysts in practice and to students and others who, for whatever reasons, are attempting to look at the world through the eyes of a practitioner.

Policy Analysis: More Art than Science

Policy analysis is more art than science. It draws on intuition as much as method. Nevertheless, given the choice between advice that imposes too much structure on the problem-solving process or too little, most beginning practitioners quite reasonably prefer too much. I have therefore developed an approach I call the Eightfold Path. The primary utility of this structured approach is that it reminds you of important tasks and choices that otherwise might slip your mind; its primary drawback is that, taken by itself, it can be mechanistic.

The Eightfold Path

Define the Problem

Assemble Some Evidence

Construct the Alternatives

Select the Criteria

Project the Outcomes

Confront the Trade-Offs

Decide!

Tell Your Story

These steps are not necessarily taken in precisely this order, nor are all of them necessarily significant in every problem. However, an effort to define the problem is usually the right starting place, and telling the story is almost inevitably the ending point. Constructing alternatives and selecting criteria for evaluating them must surely come toward the beginning of the process. Assembling some evidence is actually a step that recurs throughout the entire process, and it applies particularly to efforts to define the problem and to project the outcomes of the alternatives being considered.

Iteration Is Continual

The problem-solving process—being a process of trial and error—is iterative, so that you usually must repeat each of these steps, sometimes more than once.

The spirit in which you take any one of these steps, especially in the earliest phases of your project, should be highly tentative. As you move through the problem-solving process, you will probably keep changing your problem definition, your menu of alternatives, your set of evaluative criteria, your sense of what evidence bears on the problem, and so on. With each successive iteration you will become a bit more confident that you are on the right track, that you are focusing on the right question, and so on. This can be a frustrating process, but it can also be rewarding—provided you can learn to enjoy the challenge of search, discovery, and invention.

Some of the Guidelines Are Practical, but Most Are Conceptual

Most of the concepts used will seem obvious. However, there are exceptions. First, technical terms are sometimes employed. Second, some commonsense terms may be used in a special way that strips them of certain connotations and perhaps imports others. For the most part, all these concepts will become intelligible through experience and practice.

The Concepts Come Embedded in Concrete Particulars

In real life, policy problems appear as a confusing welter of details: personalities, interest groups, rhetorical demands, budget figures, legal rules and interpretations, bureaucratic routines, citizen attitudes, and so on. Yet the concepts described in this handbook are formulated in the abstract. You therefore need to learn to "see" the analytic concepts in the concrete manifestations of everyday life.

Your Final Product

So what will your final product look like? Here is a very rough sketch of a typical written policy-analytic report: In a coherent narrative style you will describe some problem that needs to be mitigated or solved. You will lay out a few alternative courses of action that might be taken. To each course of action you will attach a set of projected outcomes that you think your client or audience would care about, suggesting the evidentiary grounds for your projections. If no alternative dominates all other alternatives with respect to all the evaluative criteria of interest, you will indicate the nature and magnitude of the trade-offs implicit in different policy choices. Depending on the client's expectations, you might state your own recommendation as to which alternative should be chosen.

The Spirit of the Eightfold Path

The spirit of the Eightfold Path is, I hope, an economizing and uplifting spirit. Analyzing public policy problems is a complex activity. It is easy to get lost, waste a lot of time, become demoralized. Other manuals and textbooks in policy analysis are very concerned that you get the analysis "right," in some sense. I hope this one will help in that respect too. But, even more, I hope that this one will help you get it done with reasonable efficiency as well.

PART I

The Eightfold Path

1. Define the Problem

YOUR FIRST PROBLEM DEFINITION is a crucial step. It gives you (1) a reason for doing all the work necessary to complete the project and (2) a sense of direction for your evidence-gathering activity. And in the last phases of the policy analysis, your final problem definition will probably help you structure how you *tell your story.*

Usually, the raw material for your initial problem definition comes from your client and derives from the ordinary language of debate and discussion in the client's political environment, language I call generically *issue rhetoric.* This rhetoric may be narrowly confined to a seemingly technical problem or broadly located in a controversy of wide social interest. In either case, you have to get beneath the rhetoric to define a problem that is analytically manageable and that makes sense in light of the political and institutional means available for mitigating it.

Use the raw material of issue rhetoric with care. It often points to some condition of the world that people don't like or consider "bad" in some sense, like "teenage pregnancy," "media violence," or "global warming." These evaluations do not necessarily need to be taken at face value. You will sometimes wish to explore the philosophical and empirical grounds on which you, your client, or others in your eventual audience should or should not consider the alleged condition "bad." Furthermore, issue rhetoric may point to some alleged—but not necessarily real—cause of the troubling condition, for example, "welfare" or "human wastefulness." You want not simply to echo the issue rhetoric in your problem definition, but to use it as raw material for a provisional problem definition that you hope will prove analytically useful.

Some issues may connote more than one problem. Depending on the audience, for example, "teenage pregnancy" might connote sexual immorality, the blighting of young people's and their children's life chances, exploitation of taxpayers, and social disintegration. Usually you will want to determine a primary problem focus; otherwise you will find that the analysis gets out of hand. But if the problems aren't too complicated, you may feel you are willing to define more than one.

Think of Deficits and Excesses

It often—but not always—helps to think in terms of deficit and excess. For instance:

- "There are too many homeless people in the United States."
- "The demand for agricultural water is growing faster than our ability to supply it at an acceptable financial and environmental cost."
- "California's population of school-age children is growing at 140,000 per year, and our ability to develop the physical facilities in which to educate them is not growing nearly as fast."

It often helps to include the word *too* in the definition (e.g., "too big," "too small," "growing too slowly," "growing too fast"). These last two phrases (about "growing") remind us that problems deserving our attention don't necessarily exist "today" but are (at least potentially) in prospect for the future, whether near or distant.

However, it does not help to think in terms of deficit and excess when your problem is an already well-structured decision problem, for example, "Dump the dredging spoils either in the Bay or somewhere out in the Pacific Ocean." Nor does it help if your challenge is to invent *any* way to accomplish some defined objective, for example, "Find some grant funds to close the anticipated gap between revenues and expenditures." These decision- and invention-type "problems" are problems *for* the policy analyst but are not the sort of problems I am addressing in this section.

The Definition Should Be Evaluative

Remember the idea of a "problem" usually means that people think there is something wrong with the world. But note that *wrong* is a very debatable term. Not everyone will think that the facts you (or others) have defined as a problem are really a problem, for each person may apply a different evaluative framework to these facts. Unfortunately, there are no obvious or accepted ways to resolve philosophical differences of this type.

A common philosophical as well as practical question is "What private troubles warrant definition as public problems and thereby legitimately raise claims for amelioration by public resources?" It is usually helpful to view the situation through the *market failure* lens.[1] In its simplest formulation, market failure occurs when the *technical properties* of a good or service

- make it hard to collect payment from all the potential beneficiaries—for instance, the large number of people who profit, albeit indirectly, from advances in basic science;
- make it hard to collect from the beneficiaries of consumption the true economic cost of making use of the good or service—fresh air that vehicle owners use as a sink for their auto emissions;
- make it hard for consumers (and sometimes suppliers) to know the true qualities of the good or service they are acquiring—many repair-type services, including those performed by physicians as well as those performed by auto mechanics;
- make the cost of producing the marginal unit lower than the average cost within the relevant range of demand—a magazine article distributed via the Internet.

It is hard to overestimate the importance of this point, for in most—though not all—situations where no actual market failures can be identified, people's private troubles *cannot* typically be ameliorated by even the most well-intentioned governmental interventions. And even when some amelioration is possible, there are usually many adverse side effects. In some cases, it may nevertheless be worthwhile to pay the price of these side effects, but such calculations must be done carefully and scrupulously.

Besides market failures, the main situations where private troubles can warrant definition as public problems are

- breakdowns of systems, such as family relationships, that occur largely outside markets;
- the concern of many citizens about low living standards that arise precisely *because* markets function well and do not reward individuals very generously if they lack marketable assets;

---

1. See chapter 5 in David L. Weimar and Aidan R. Vining, *Policy Analysis: Concepts and Practice* (Upper Saddle River, N.J.: Prentice Hall, 1999). For a persuasive analysis of most traditional market failures in transaction cost terms, see Richard O. Zerbe Jr., and Howard E. McCurdy, "The Failure of Market Failure," *Journal of Policy Analysis and Management* 18, no. 4 (1999): 558–78. Zerbe and McCurdy also emphasize the rich variety of interventions besides those undertaken by government to remedy traditionally conceived "market failures."

- the existence of discrimination against racial and other minorities;
- the failure of government to function well in areas where it is traditionally expected to act effectively (e.g., in providing public schools).

Quantify If Possible

The definition should, insofar as possible, include a quantitative feature. Assertions of deficit or excess should come with *magnitudes* attached. How big is "too big"? How small is "too small"? How about "too slowly"? How about "too fast"? In the examples above, how many homeless people are there in the United States? How many acre-feet of water are used now, and how does that amount compare with the demand in some specified future year (given certain assumptions about water pricing)? Exactly what is "our ability to develop physical facilities," and how do we expect it to grow, or shrink, over time?

If necessary, gather information to help you calibrate the relevant magnitudes. See the discussion under "Assemble Some Evidence."

In many or most cases, you will have to estimate—or "guesstimate," more likely—the magnitudes in question. Sometimes you should furnish a *range* as well as a *point* estimate of magnitudes (e.g., "Our best guess of the number of homeless persons in families is 250,000, although the truth could lie between 100,000 and 400,000").

Conditions That Cause Problems Are Also Problems

Some problem conditions are not experienced as troublesome per se by citizens but are perceived by them, or by analysts working on their behalf, to be causes of troubles. It is sometimes useful to diagnose one or more alleged causes of this type and to define these as problems to be mitigated or removed, for instance, "One of the problems in the air pollution area is that states have not been willing to force motorists to keep their engines tuned up and their exhaust systems in proper order."

Note that this sort of problem definition is not merely descriptive but is also *diagnostic*. It implicitly asserts that some condition, which may or may not be troubling to people per se, is an important *cause* of some other condition that is indeed troubling. Problem definitions that pretend to some diagnostic power can be useful, but they can also be treacherous. Suppose, after all, that the causal diagnosis is mistaken or misleading, for example, that states' unwillingness to enforce engine maintenance routines is *not* in fact a very important cause of air pollution. Because *definition* in some contexts connotes legitimate arbitrariness ("I'll define 'justice' to mean . . .") the causal claims implicit in diagnostic problem definitions can easily escape needed scrutiny. See "Project the Outcomes" for further discussion.

Missing an Opportunity Is a Problem

A special case of "a problem" is an opportunity missed. Is it not rather small-minded to think of policy analysis as devoted merely to the amelioration of "problems"? May policy analysis not rise above the tedious and uninspiring business of patching and fixing? Can we not aspire to a world in which we can identify opportunities to do creative—not to say wonderful—things? "If it ain't broke, don't fix it" is a confining idea, and certainly policy analysts, policymakers, and public managers ought not to allow the "problem" focus to restrict the search for plausible opportunities. Unfortunately, the working agenda of most policy professionals is set by complaints, threats, worries, and troubles. There is often little time or energy left over to think about improvements that no one has identified as missing. Still, if latent opportunities are really lying around, it would be a pity to ignore them.

Where do we find opportunities for creative policy improvements that haven't first been identified by complaints, threats, and so on? Little academic or technical theory is available to answer this question. But Box I.I (p. 6) contains a list that is suggestive.

Common Pitfalls in Problem Definition

Problem definition is a deceptively simple step. It is a step beset by at least two dangerous pitfalls.

Defining the solution into the "problem." Your problem definition should not include an implicit solution introduced by semantic carelessness. Projected solutions must be evaluated empirically and not legitimated merely by definition. Therefore, keep the problem definition stripped down to a mere description, and leave open where you will look for solutions.

- *Don't say:* "There is too little shelter for homeless families." This formulation might inadvertently imply that "more shelter" is the best solution and might inhibit you from thinking about ways to prevent families from becoming homeless in the first place. *Try instead:* "There are too many homeless families."
- *Don't say:* "New schools are being built too slowly." This formulation could imply "more schools" as the solution and could inhibit you from thinking about ways to use existing facilities more efficiently. *Try instead:*

BOX I.I.   SOME GENERIC OPPORTUNITIES FOR SOCIAL IMPROVEMENT THAT OFTEN GO UNNOTICED

By-products of personal aspirations. It is possible to structure new incentives or create new opportunities for personal advantage or satisfaction that can indirectly result in social benefit (e.g., offering to share the benefits of cost-reducing innovations with public sector employees who conceive them and implement them).

Complementarity. Two or more activities can be joined so that each makes the other more productive (e.g., public works construction and combating unemployment).

Development. A sequence of activities or operations may have the potential to be arranged to take advantage of a developmental process (e.g., assessing welfare clients for employability and vocational interest before, rather than after, sending them out on a job search).

Exchange. There are unrealized possibilities for exchange that would increase social value. We typically design policies to exploit those that simulate market-like arrangements (e.g., pollution permit auctions, and arrangements to reimburse an agency for services it renders another agency's clients or customers).

Multiple functions. A system can be designed so that one feature can be used to perform two or more functions (e.g., when a tax administrator dramatizes an enforcement case in such a way as both to deter potential violators and to reassure nonviolators that they are not being made into suckers for their honesty).

Nontraditional participants. Line-level employees of public agencies often have knowledge of potential program improvements that could usefully be incorporated into the agencies' policies and operations. The same is true of the agencies' customers or clients or the parties that they regulate.

Rationalization. Purely technical rationalization of a system is possible (e.g., shortening queues by deliberate spacing of arrival times, or creating contracts to solidify informal agreements that are vulnerable to decay and misunderstanding).

Rummaging. By rummaging mentally, one might discover novel uses in seemingly improbable but readily available materials (e.g., using the automobile registration system as a vehicle for carrying out voter registration as well).

Underutilized capacity. An example, in many communities, is school facilities that are utilized for relatively limited purposes for only part of the day and for only part of the year—although school officials would be quick to warn that using this capacity without harming school functions is not always easy.

"There are too many schoolchildren relative to the currently available classroom space."

A tipoff that you're probably smuggling an implicit solution into the problem definition is to hear yourself saying, "Aha, but that's not the real problem; the real problem is . . ." While there are better and worse ways to conceptualize a problem, or to solve a problem, it stretches ordinary usage too much to say that one problem could be "more (less) real" than another.

Be skeptical about the causal claims implicit in diagnostic problem definitions. I said above that "conditions that cause problems are also problems." However, the causes must be real, not merely assumed. You have to evaluate the causal chain that goes from the situation itself to the bad things it is alleged to cause, and to convince yourself that the causal chain is real. For instance, for some people, "cocaine use" is not a problem in itself, but it might be a problem if it *leads to* crime, poor health, family disintegration, and so on. But does it lead to these outcomes, and to what degree? The evidence on this question should be evaluated very carefully before you decide it's okay to work with a problem definition involving "too much cocaine use."

Iterate

Problem definition is a crucial step. But because it is hard to get it right, you might take that same step again and again. Over the course of your analytic work, your empirical and conceptual understanding will evolve. Also, as you begin to rule out alternative approaches to solving or mitigating your problem, you will probably want to sculpt the problem definition so that, in the end, you and the political system will have some chance of attacking the problem successfully. Finally, if you are working in an office or agency context, you will implicitly be negotiating a mutually acceptable problem definition with your analyst colleagues and your hierarchical superiors.[2]

2. Assemble Some Evidence

All of your time doing a policy analysis is spent in two activities: thinking (sometimes aloud and sometimes with others) and hustling data that can be

---

2. Some analysts also claim that it is simply not worthwhile to define as "problems" conditions that cannot be ameliorated: "Problems are better treated as opportunities for improvement; defined problems, as problems of choice between alternative means to realize a given opportunity. The process of problem definition would then be one of search, creation, and initial examination of ideas for solution until a problem of choice is reached." David Dery, *Problem Definition in Policy Analysis* (Lawrence: University Press of Kansas, 1984), 27.

turned into evidence. Of these two activities, thinking is by far the more important, but hustling data takes much more time: reading documents, hunting in libraries, poring over studies and statistics, interviewing people, traveling to interviews and waiting for appointments, and so on.

The real-world settings in which policy analysis is done rarely afford the time for a research effort that would please a careful academic researcher. In fact, time pressure is probably almost as dangerous an enemy of high-quality policy analysis as politically motivated bias, if not more so. Therefore, it is essential to economize on your data collection activities. The key to economizing is this: Try to collect only those data that can be turned into "information" that, in turn, can be converted into "evidence" that has some bearing on your problem.

For the logically minded, here are some definitions: *Data* are facts—or, some might say, representations of facts—about the world. Data include all sorts of statistics but go well beyond statistics, too. Data also include, for instance, facts about an agency manager's ability to deal constructively with the press. *Information* is data that has "meaning," in the sense that it can help you sort the world into different logical or empirical categories. The prevalence of cigarette smoking in five different countries is data, but these data become information when you decide it is interesting to array the countries comparatively (e.g., from lowest to highest prevalence). *Evidence* is information that affects the existing beliefs of important people (including yourself) about significant features of the problem you are studying and how it might be solved or mitigated. Differential prevalence of smoking, for instance, can become evidence bearing on hypotheses about differential levels of concern about personal health across countries.

You need evidence for three principal purposes. One purpose is to assess the nature and extent of the problem(s) you are trying to define. A second is to assess the particular features of the concrete policy situation you are engaged in studying. For instance, you may need to know—or guess—about agency workloads, recent budget figures, demographic changes in a service area, the political ideology of the agency chief, the competency of the middle-level managers in the agency, and the current attitudes of some other agency that nominally cooperates with this one on some problem. The third purpose is to assess policies that have been thought, by at least some people, to have worked effectively in situations apparently similar to your own, in other jurisdictions, perhaps, or at other times.[3] All three purposes are relevant to the goal of producing realistic projections of possible policy outcomes.

Because each of these purposes becomes salient in different phases of the

---

3. Sometimes these situations will have been evaluated statistically, and sometimes not: see Part III, "'Smart (Best) Practices' Research."

policy analysis process, this "Assemble Some Evidence" step on the Eightfold Path will be taken more than once, but with a different focus each time.

Think Before You Collect

Thinking and collecting data are complementary activities: you can be a much more efficient collector of data if you think, and keep on thinking, about what you do and don't need (or want) to know, and why. The principal—and exceedingly common—mistake made by beginners and veterans alike is to spend time collecting data that have little or no potential to be developed into evidence concerning anything you actually care about. People often do this because running around collecting data looks and feels productive whereas first-rate thinking is hard and frustrating. Also, the people paying for your work tend to be reassured that, when they see you busily collecting data, somehow they are getting their money's worth.

The value of evidence. Since most evidence is costly to produce, you must weigh its likely cost against its likely value. How is its likely value to be estimated? The answer may be cast in a decision-analytic framework (decision trees), though you should remember that the process of making a decision involves a great many elements prior to the moment of actual choice, such as defining a useful problem, thinking up better candidate solutions, and selecting a useful model. In general, the value of any piece of evidence depends on

- the likelihood that it will cause you to substitute some better decision for whatever decision you would have made without it (which might have been an "acceptable" decision in and of itself);
- the likelihood that the substituted decision will, directly or indirectly, produce a better policy outcome than the outcome that would have been produced by the original decision;
- the magnitude of the difference in value between the likely-to-be improved outcome and the original outcome.

Self-control. It is surprising how well you can do in many cases by gathering no evidence at all but simply sitting down and thinking something through and then making some serious educated guesses. There is nothing shameful about acting on such guesstimates and thereby conserving your data-collecting time and energies for answering questions for which good evidence is really necessary. See Part II, "Gathering Data for Policy Research."

A helpful check on yourself, to prevent yourself from collecting useless data, is to ask yourself the following questions before embarking on some data collection venture:

- "Suppose the data turn out to look like so-and-so as opposed to thus-and-such. What implication would that have for my understanding of how to solve this problem?"
- "Compared to my best guess about how the data will look once I've got them, how much different might they look if I actually took the trouble to get them?"
- "How much is it worth to me to confirm the actual difference between what I can guess and what I can learn about the world by really getting the data?"

It is this sort of critical attitude about the value of expensive data collection that often leads good and experienced policy analysts to make do with back-of-the-envelope estimates. However, none of the above is meant to be an excuse for shirking the job of getting good data—and sometimes lots of them, at huge costs in time and money—when you've convinced yourself that the investment really would pay off. There's an obvious and critical difference between justifiable and unjustifiable guesstimates.

Do a Literature Review

There is hardly a problem without some academic discipline or professional association doing research on its causes and solutions. It is easy to find journals and various professional publications disseminating research results, theories, case studies, the musings of experienced practitioners, and so on. The Internet brings much of this to your desktop, but some of the best vehicles are better accessed by browsing the periodical shelves of university or government libraries.

Advocacy organizations often publish a great deal of interesting work and may take special pains to disseminate their work on the Internet. However, there is a danger of relying too much on such sources just because they are readily available.

Survey "Best Practice"

The chances are that the problem you are studying is not unique, and that policymakers and public managers in other jurisdictions, perhaps not very different from the one you are studying, have dealt with it in some fashion. See if you can track down some of these past solutions and see if you can extrapolate them to the situation you are studying. The extrapolation process is complicated, though. See Part III, "'Smart (Best) Practices' Research: Understanding and Making Use of What Look like Good Ideas from Somewhere Else."

Use Analogies

Sometimes it pays to gather data about things that are, on the surface, quite unlike the problem you are studying but that, under the surface, show instructive similarities. For instance, your understanding of how a merit pay plan for compensating managers in the public sector might work could perhaps be improved by seeing how similar schemes work in the private sector. Or if you are working on the problem of how a state can discipline, and perhaps disbar, incompetent attorneys, you might usefully spend a good deal of your time learning about how the medical profession handles problems of physician incompetence. If you are working on how to reduce neighborhoods' resistance to accepting low-income housing projects, you could usefully look into the literature on community resistance to accepting solid-waste incinerators.

As these examples suggest, some analogies are easier to perceive, and to make sense of, than others. It takes a little imagination to see instructive analogies and, occasionally, a little daring to try to convince others to see both the usefulness of the analogy and its inevitable limitations.

Start Early

You are often dependent on the busy schedules of other very busy people whom you ask to furnish you with information or opportunities for interviews. It is extremely important to put in requests for information, especially interviews, well in advance of when you expect to want to have completed the data collection.[4]

Touching Base, Gaining Credibility, Brokering Consensus

The process of assembling evidence inevitably has a political as well as a purely analytical purpose. Sometimes it entails touching base with potential critics of your work so that they will not be able to complain that you ignored their perspectives. By making yourself known to potential supporters of your work, you may also be able to create a cadre of defenders.

A more complex objective, where appropriate, might be to blend policy analysis with the process of improving a policy idea or decision during the course of implementation. (See the following discussion of "improvability" as a criterion.) This entails obtaining "feedback" from participants, usually in an iterative process,

---

4. For a useful description of how to conduct literature reviews, library searches, phone interviews, and personal interviews, see Weimer and Vining, *Policy Analysis,* chap. 10A. See also Part II, "Gathering Data for Policy Research."

and sharing some of your own reactions with them. You become more of a partner in the process than an outside observer and diagnostician. An even more complex and challenging role is for you to become a particular type of "partner," a facilitator and broker, whether by acting as a transmission belt from one person to another or by convening meetings and other gatherings.

Freeing the Captive Mind

In exchange for access to data and a ready-made worldview, researchers sometimes uncritically accept problem definitions and preferred solutions from kindly informants (not to mention from paying clients or employers). To counter such temptations, be sure to make contact with individuals or factions whom you would expect to disagree—the more sharply the better—with your kindly informants. A time-saving, but only partial, substitute is to ask your kindly informant, "Who might object strongly to your point of view about this, and why might they do so?"

3. Construct the Alternatives

By *alternatives* I mean something like "policy options," or "alternative courses of action," or "alternative strategies of intervention to solve or mitigate the problem."

Start Comprehensive, End Up Focused

In the last stages of your analysis, you won't want to be assessing more than three or four principal alternatives. But in the beginning, you should err on the side of comprehensiveness: Make a list of all the alternatives you might wish to consider in the course of your analysis. Later on you will discard some obvious losers, combine others, and reorganize still others into a single "basic" alternative with one or more subsidiary "variants." For your initial list, though, where should you turn for ideas?

- Note the alternatives that key political actors are actively proposing or seem to have on their minds. These may include people's pet ideas, institutions' inventories of "off-the-shelf" proposals that simply await a window of opportunity, and prepackaged proposals that political ideologues are perennially advocating.

- Try to *invent* alternatives that might prove to be superior to the alternatives currently being discussed by the key political actors. It's good to brainstorm, to try to be creative—but don't expect that you'll necessarily produce much better ideas than other people have already thought about. One way to coax your creativity is to refer to the checklist in Appendix A, "Things Governments Do." For each entry on the list, ask yourself, "Might it make sense to try some version of this generic strategy to help mitigate this problem?"[5] Because it is a long and comprehensive list, the answer with respect to any single strategy will usually be negative. Going through the list systematically is worthwhile, however. Because the list is not very long, with experience you will need to spend only a few minutes to decide whether any ideas there might be worth considering further.
- Always include in your first approach to the problem the alternative "Let present trends continue undisturbed." You need to do this because the world is full of naturally occurring change, and some of these ongoing changes might mitigate the problem on which you are working. (Note that I am not characterizing this alternative as "Do Nothing." It is not possible to "do nothing." Most of the trends in motion will probably persist and alter the problem, whether for better or for worse.)

In most cases, however, this "let-present-trends-continue" option will drop out of your final analysis. This happens because, if you do your problem definition work well, you will end up with an important problem in your sights that in most cases can be mitigated to some degree by some affirmative action.

Inspect the most common sources of "natural" change in the public policy environment to see if any will affect the scope of the problem:

1. Political changes following elections, as well as changes induced by the prospects of having to contest an election
2. Changes in unemployment and inflation rates that accompany the business cycle
3. The changing "tightness" or "looseness" of agency budgets caused by overall taxing and spending policies
4. Demographic changes, such as population migration patterns and population "bulges" moving through certain ages.

---

5. See also the very valuable discussion on generic policy instruments in Weimer and Vining, *Policy Analysis,* chap. 9.

Model the System in Which the Problem Is Located

We often think about alternative approaches to the problem as possible *interventions* in the system that holds the problem in place or keeps it going. Logically, it is not necessary to model the causes of a problem in order to cure it—pharmaceutical manufacturers can testify that many of their successful products work by unknown causal routes on conditions whose causes are not at all understood. But a good causal model is often quite useful for suggesting possible "intervention points." This is especially true when the problem is embedded in a complex system of interacting forces, incentives, and constraints—which is usually the case. Consider, for instance, a system that produces "too much traffic congestion" at some choke point like a bridge or a tunnel. A sketch of the relevant causal model would include the demand for travel along the relevant route, the available modes of travel, the amount of roadway capacity, and the price to users of roadway capacity. An efficient and simple—but usually politically unpopular—intervention might be to increase the price to users so as to reflect the degree to which each user contributes to congestion and increased travel times.

How elaborate, rigorous, and self-conscious should your causal model be? Many social scientists who devote themselves to policy analysis would hold, "The more the better." I say, "Yes, but . . ." Self-consciousness is highly desirable. Elaborateness (or comprehensiveness, in this case a near synonym) is desirable because it decreases the risk of missing important causal connections. But it can blur the analytic focus and blunt creativity in designing intervention strategies. Rigor is desirable if it prevents you from relying on unarticulated and false assumptions. But its down side is that you might exclude factors that are important—for instance, the personalities of certain actors—because you don't know how to model their effect rigorously and/or because you have only hunches regarding the nature of the relevant personalities.

Many models are best thought of as elaborations of some fundamental metaphor. Some elaborations can be mathematical and quite precise, while others are verbal and evocative. Some commonly used metaphors that are the bases for models of particular value in designing alternatives are discussed here:

- *A market where disaggregated suppliers exchange goods or services with disaggregated demanders.* Note that market models can apply to unpriced goods and services. The main idea behind the market model is really equilibration through exchange. Hence, the market model can be applied to many phenomena other than the production and allocation of textbook goods like widgets or apples.

  For instance, you might try to understand the flow of patients into a state mental hospital system in terms of supply and demand: there is a short-run "supply" of available beds in state hospitals and a per-diem charge for each, while there is a complex "demand" for their use generated by police departments, county psychiatric emergency units, judges, members of the public, and so on.

A standard intervention strategy for improving markets that are not working as well as they might be is to find some way to raise or lower the prices faced by either suppliers or demanders.

- *Production models.* Unfortunately, there is not much of an academic literature about the operating logics of the common types of production systems found in public policy (e.g., command-and-control regulation, the provision of information, and all those other "Things Governments Do" briefly described in Appendix A).[6] In any case, the main concern in understanding production systems should be to identify the parameters whose values, when they move out of a certain range, make the systems most vulnerable to breakdown, fraud and abuse, egregious diseconomies, and the distortion of intended purpose. It is also helpful to know about those parameters that matter most when we try to upgrade a production system from mere adequacy to performance levels we might think of as "excellent." (See Part III on smart practices.)

Another way to look at production models is through optimization lenses. Operations research models (e.g., queuing, inventory management, Markov processes) are relevant here.[7]

- *Evolutionary models,* constructed of three important subprocesses: variation among competitors, selection, and retention. Suppose, for instance, that, in an agency enforcing health-related standards in the workplace, the complaints disproportionately concerned visible and annoying problems which were not, however, as hazardous to worker health as less visible and annoying problems. In this case, the evolutionary model suggests several plausible intervention points. The agency might try to educate workers to detect and complain about more serious problems, and try thereby to swamp the less serious problems (thus changing the pool of "competitors"). It might start screening the complaints for their likelihood of being associated with more fruitful targets (thus changing the se-

---

6. However, see chapter 9 on "generic policies" in Weimer and Vining, *Policy Analysis.* Also see Lester Salamon, ed., *Beyond Privatization: The Tools of Government Action* (Washington, D.C.: Urban Institute Press, 1989).
7. For a good, brief discussion, see Stokey and Zeckhauser, *A Primer,* and Andres G. Victorio, *Applied Models in Public Policy* (Manila: Ateneo de Manila University, 1995). Also see the models, particularly that of case management, in Stephen R. Rosenthal, *Managing Government Operations* (Boston: Little, Brown, 1982).

lection mechanism). Or it might attempt to persuade workers, and perhaps their union representatives, to reduce their propensity to complain about matters the agency wishes to hear less about (thus changing the "retention mechanism," workers' attitudes).[8]

Reduce and Simplify the List of Alternatives

The final list of alternatives—the one you include in your presentation to your client and other audiences—will almost certainly look quite different from the one you started with. Not only will you have thrown some out that just don't look very good, but you will also have done some work to *conceptualize* and *simplify* alternatives.

The key to conceptualization is to try to sum up the basic strategic thrust of an alternative in a simple sentence or even a phrase. This is difficult but usually worth the effort. It usually helps to use very plain, short phrases stripped of jargon. When the Environmental Protection Agency (EPA) was created, the first administrator confronted (a partial list of) alternatives that might have been described thus: "Let the states do the work; let the feds give them the money"; "Remove impediments to firms cooperating on antipollution research"; and "Sue the bastards" (meaning the large, visible polluting firms and industries, the prosecution of which would help build political support for the new agency).

The key to simplification is to distinguish between a basic alternative and its variants. The basic element in many policy alternatives is an intervention strategy, such as regulatory enforcement or a subsidy or a tax incentive, that causes people or institutions to change their conduct in some way.[9] But no intervention strategy can stand alone; it must be implemented by some agency or constellation of agencies (perhaps including nonprofit organizations), and it must have a source of financing. Usually the variants on the basic strategy are defined by different methods of implementation and different methods of financing.

The distinction between a basic strategy and variants based on implementation details is especially helpful when you have a lot of possible solutions to consider and you need to reduce the complexity involved in comparing them. Making

8. For other ideas and an excellent discussion of the uses of models generally, see Charles A. Lave and James G. March, *An Introduction to Models in the Social Sciences* (New York: Harper and Row, 1975).

9. Often, though not always, the basic element is something like a smart practice, that is, an intervention strategy that attempts to take advantage of some qualitative opportunity to create valued change at relatively low cost and/or risk. See Part III, "'Smart (Best) Practices' Research."

the distinction puts you in a position to break your analysis into successive steps. In the first step you might compare three "basic" alternatives, say, while ignoring the details described by their "variants." Then, once you have decided on one of these "basic" alternatives, you would turn to comparing the variants. Here are two examples:

- You want to decrease the prevalence of heroin use in your county by 50 percent over the next five years. You consider three basic alternatives: methadone maintenance, law enforcement pressure, and drug education. Variants for each one have to do with the funding sources, in that state, federal, and county money can be used in different degrees (although not all mixes of funds available for one approach are also available for the other two). Variation is also possible according to who administers the program(s): nonprofit organizations, county employees, or state employees.
- You can also consider variants of scale and scope. You might wish to consider two possible sizes for your methadone program, for instance.

Design Problems

This handbook assumes throughout that you are working on a problem of policy choice. However, a special case of policy choice occurs when you wish to, or have to, *design* at least one policy alternative to put into the menu of possibilities. Perhaps you are just not satisfied with the menu of alternatives that people in the policy environment are already talking about. Or perhaps the problem you are dealing with is so new or unique that you will be the first, or even the only, person to oversee the needed design work.

Consider what is involved in designing a house, an office building, a living room, a dance production, a theater set, a fund-raising event, a political campaign, a graduate public policy curriculum, a nonprofit environmental education organization to operate on a national scale, or a profit-seeking organization to manufacture and market cyberwidgets in ten to twenty national markets. Clearly, design is a complex process, requiring many iterations, in which you both explore different ways to accomplish a certain set of objectives and alter the set of objectives in light of what you learn about what is actually practicable.

In some cases, the policy analyst works on the design problem more or less alone, like some brooding master architect. More likely she does her work in loose or tight conjunction with other policy professionals who bring different sorts of expertise (e.g., legal, engineering, fiscal) to the table, and who bring different viewpoints and priorities as well. In any case, sooner or later, the design work will be held out for much more public view. Interested stakeholders, and perhaps the general public, who have previously been unaware of the design work going on seemingly behind the scenes, will see what you're up to. And they will make their comments. The comments—sometimes explicit, sometimes transmitted in body language or other code—will approximate these five types:

- "Great work. Keep it up; we're for it."
- "We're for it provided you make the following changes: . . . Otherwise, we're against it."
- "We're for it provided you don't cave in to those who will seek changes in . . ."
- "It's awful, 'dead-on-arrival.'"
- "We can hardly believe the undemocratic way in which you've excluded us, but we can be mollified if . . ."

You will want to use such reactions for two purposes: to improve your design according to criteria which you and your client think are important, including the criterion of political feasibility, and to respond in such a way as to increase the political support (and decrease the opposition) that come your way, now or later, on process grounds alone. I shall not discuss here the strategy and tactics involved in how to communicate with different audiences or the sequence in which to do so. I limit discussion to the question of just how *rough* or *polished* the design should be that you first subject to relatively public review and comment.

Not surprisingly, a middle ground is best. A very rough design may leave out important points, creating a sort of vacuum that outside interests will rush to fill on their own terms. You will then be forced onto the defensive, as you try to forestall the solution they have been first to suggest. Moreover, a very rough design might signal that the design work is at such a preliminary stage that it is not worth the trouble (or the risk of early-mover vulnerability) for any of the stakeholders to react at all. On the other hand, an overly polished design might signal stakeholders that you are not interested in consulting them. In that case, they might feel that they have no choice but to oppose your design more vehemently than they otherwise might have done—unless, of course, they conclude that they have no choice but to get onboard and negotiate for the best terms they can manage.

Assuming you put out a rough-but-not-too-rough design and elicit a range of fairly thoughtful opinion as a result, you will need ways to keep in touch with the variety of actors who now expect—and whom you may wish—to be part of an ongoing, if rather diffuse, design process. Keeping in touch implies a communications infrastructure (telephone, fax machine, e-mail), of course. It also implies efforts on your part to develop the sort of network relationships that permit rapid and reasonably trustworthy interpersonal communications.

A Linguistic Pitfall

Alternative does not necessarily signify that the policy options are mutually exclusive. Policy analysts use the term *alternative* ambiguously. Sometimes it means that choosing an alternative implies forgoing another, and sometimes it means simply one more policy action that might help solve or mitigate some problem, perhaps in conjunction with other alternatives. You should be aware of the ambiguity in other people's usage, and in telling your story (Step 8), you should be sure that no such ambiguity enters your own usage.

Sometimes you won't be entirely sure whether two alternatives are or are not mutually exclusive. For instance, the mayor might have promised enough money to either fix potholes or provide homeless shelters (but not both), but you may have made such a great case for both programs that the mayor might decide to increase the budgetary allocation.

4. Select the Criteria

It helps to think of any policy story (see Step 8) as having two interconnected but separable plot lines, the analytical and the evaluative. The first is all about facts and disinterested projections of consequences, while the second is all about value judgments. Ideally, all analytically sophisticated and open-minded persons can agree, more or less, on the rights and wrongs in the analytical plot and on the nature of its residual uncertainties. But this is not true with regard to the evaluative plot—where we expect subjectivity and social philosophy to cavort more freely. The analytical plot will reason about whether X, Y, or Z is likely to happen, but it is in the evaluative plot that we learn whether we think X or Y or Z good or bad for the world.

The step in the Eightfold Path called "Select the criteria" belongs to the evaluative plot line. It is the most important step for permitting values and philosophy to be brought into the policy analysis, because criteria are evaluative standards used to judge the goodness of the projected policy outcomes associated with each of the alternatives.

Apply Evaluative Criteria to Judging Outcomes, Not Alternatives

Please note that evaluative criteria are *not* used to judge the alternatives, or at least not directly. They are to be applied to the projected outcomes. It is easy to get confused about this point—and to get the analysis very tangled as a result. This confusion is encouraged by a commonsense way of speaking: "Alternative A looks to be the best; therefore let's proceed with it." But this way of speaking ignores a very important step. The complete formulation is "Alternative A will very probably lead to outcome O_A, which we judge to be the best of the possible outcomes; therefore, we judge Alternative A to be the best." Applying criteria to the evaluation of outcomes and not of alternatives makes it possible to remember that we might like O_A a great deal even if, because we lack sufficient confidence that A would actually lead to O_A, we decide not to choose Alternative A after all. With that judgment on the table, it would be possible to look for other alternatives with a greater likelihood of producing O_A.

Criteria Selection Builds on Problem Definition—and Continues

Of course, the most important evaluative criterion is that the projected outcome will solve the policy problem to an acceptable degree. But this is only the beginning. After all, any course of action is likely to affect the world in many ways, some desired and some not. Each of those effects—or projected outcomes, to return to our Eightfold Path language—requires a judgment on our part as to whether and why it is thought desirable. Our set of criteria embodies such judgments. Because any significant impact cries out for such a judgment to be made, the greater the variety of significant impacts, the richer will be the set of evaluative criteria we will need to deal with them.

Evaluative Criteria Commonly Used in Policy Analysis

Efficiency. Typically, the efficiency criterion is the most important evaluative consideration in cost-effectiveness and cost-benefit studies. I use *efficiency* more or less as the term is used in economics, for maximizing the aggregate of individuals' welfare as *welfare* would be construed by the individuals themselves: in economic jargon, "Maximize the sum of individual utilities," or "Maximize net benefits."

Note that although *efficiency* has an antiseptic, technocratic, and elitist ring to it, the insistence here that *utility* is to be assessed according to individual citizens' construction of their own welfare is thoroughly democratic. Indeed, siding with efficiency—on average, across most policy issues and policy decisions—is a way to produce more humanistic policy results, too. The reason is not that efficiency is so very humane, but that policy decisions failing to consider efficiency very often fail to take account of the welfare of the little guy at all. The little guy may be little, but in a proper efficiency analysis, he at least shows up to be counted. Efficiency analysis imposes a moral check (for whatever that is worth in the real world of politics) on political visionaries eager to relocate entire populations so as to make room for dams, and on special interests eager to impose seemingly small price increases on large numbers of consumers through protectionist measures in order to maintain the incomes of a relatively small number of producers.

We should observe, though, that from the point of view of social justice, the efficiency criterion might be somewhat limited. First, because analysts typically estimate people's "utility" by inferring their willingness to pay money for some benefit (or to be spared some deprivation), people with less money do not, in an analytical sense, have as much clout as those with more. Just how big a limitation this analytical anti-egalitarianism turns out to be will depend on particular cases, however. Second, if the values at stake have few or no human defenders, and therefore no human pocketbooks to back an estimate of willingness to pay, the efficiency criterion might underestimate these values even if by some conception of justice they ought to be weighted heavily. In theory, ecological values are the main example, although in fact some ecological values do have human defenders who derive enormous utility from preserving them, a utility that would be accounted for in a proper efficiency analysis.

Although cost-effectiveness (CE) analysis and benefit-cost (BC) analysis sound alike and are frequent traveling companions, they are not the same, and their uses can be quite different. True, both conceptualize a domain of benefits accruing to individual citizens valued in terms of their utility. And both construe the policy problem as involving some production relationship between resources and welfare-increasing outcomes. However, CE takes one or the other of these (either resources or outcomes) as fixed or targeted; the analysis then tries to find the best means to manipulate the other one (either maximizing the benefits given the level of assumed resources or minimizing the number of resources given the targeted outcome requirement). BC, on the other hand, allows both resources and outcomes to be treated as variable in scale. It is therefore more complicated than CE, for while both BC and CE concern themselves with the productive efficiency of the program or project, BC is additionally concerned with the program's scale.

CE analysis is much more common than BC analysis. Indeed, a surprisingly large number of policy issues can be simplified and stylized as CE problems, even though on the surface they may not appear to be likely candidates at all for this sort of treatment, for example:

- The Mudville mayor wishes to respond to business complaints that building permits "take forever" to obtain. The CE framework might suggest minimizing delay arising from purely procedural and bureaucratic sources, given that you can spend no more than $500 and are permitted to change the work flow in the city planning office, but not personnel assignments.

- Quake City must upgrade the seismic safety of several thousand buildings constructed of unreinforced masonry. You have a twenty-year time span and no immediate budget constraint, but you wish to accomplish the job with minimum disruption to the lives (and incomes) of the residents and small businesses that may be temporarily displaced by the building renovation process.

Equality, equity, fairness, "justice." There are, of course, a great many different, and often opposed, ideas about what these terms do, or should, mean. Not only ought you yourself to think hard about these ideas, but sometimes you should also take your audience through some of that thinking.

- In California, drivers who do not carry liability insurance leave persons whom they injure in auto accidents at risk of being undercompensated. Many of those who "go bare" are relatively poor. Many other drivers purchase their own insurance against exactly this risk ("uninsured-motorist coverage"). A policy proposal to pay for all drivers' liability insurance out of a fund created by surcharges at the fuel pump was denounced by some observers as "inequitable" to the poor, who currently go bare of insurance. Other observers said that those who go bare impose inequitable premium expenses or risks of undercompensation on the rest of society, including many individuals who are themselves poor or not very well off. Clearly the analyst needs to include a discussion of the idea of equity.
- The current debate over whether to retain affirmative action preferences in university admissions for African-Americans and certain other minorities is sometimes said to pit fairness to individuals against justice to social groups. This is odd, though, since some philosophers and most ordinary folk, too, suppose that no system claiming to be just could contain any features deemed unfair. Again, the analyst has a job to do in sorting out ideas and language.

Freedom, community, and other ideas. To stimulate thought, here is a (far from complete) list with more ideas about evaluative criteria of possible relevance: free markets, economic freedom, capitalism, "freedom from government control," equality of opportunity, equality of result, free speech, religious freedom, privacy, safety (especially from chemicals, various environmental hazards, etc.), neighborliness, community, sense of belonging, order, security, absence of fear, traditional

family structure, egalitarian family structure, empowerment of workers, maintenance of a viable nonprofit sector, voluntarism.

Weighting Conflicting Evaluative Criteria

As we saw in the case of defining the problem, when values are at issue, as they
are in regard to criterion selection, too, we must reckon how to weight opposing
values. There are two general approaches to this problem.

The political process takes care of it. One approach is simply to allow
existing governmental and political processes to make the weighting. Typically, this
approach will accord primacy to the analyst's employer or client, with derivative
influence exercised by those parties in the relevant arena who are in turn important
to the employer or client.

The analyst imposes a solution. A second approach is for the analyst himself
or herself to modify—though not replace—the weighting accorded by the employer
or client by reference to some overarching philosophical and political conception.
The justification usually offered for this approach is that because certain interests,
and perhaps philosophies, are typically "underrepresented" in government and
politics, and because the analyst is in a better position than most other participants
in the process to see or understand or appreciate this problem of underrepresenta-
tion, the analyst is duty-bound, or at least permitted, in the name of fairness and
democracy, to right the balance.

For instance, some would argue that were it not for policy analysts, efficiency-
related criteria would rarely be heeded and that as a consequence, analysts should
in effect speak up for the taxpayers whose interests would be squeezed out by
better organized advocacy groups. A related argument is sometimes made that
certain conceptions of equity—in particular those having to do with the idea that
the beneficiaries of publicly provided goods or services should pay for them—are
underrepresented except among policy analysts. (This conception of equity normally excludes public expenditures deliberately intended to redistribute wealth
among citizens.) Other interests that people sometimes claim are underrepresented
and therefore need representation by analysts are future generations, children,
people who live outside the jurisdiction making the decisions, ethnic and racial
minorities, women, the poor, consumers, and animals and plants (ecological
entities).

A variant of this approach introduces the idea of an educational process.
Depending on circumstances, the analyst might encourage influential political
parties—perhaps including the analyst's boss or principal client—to rethink their
existing criteria in the light of facts or arguments the analyst can draw to their

attention. In this case the analyst is responsible for opening up a dialogue, and perhaps for trying to infuse it with reason and insight, but then allows the political process to take over.

Practical Criteria

Not all criteria that come into play in an analysis are part of the evaluative plot line. Some are purely practical and are part of the analytical plot line. These have to do with what happens to an alternative as it moves through the policy adoption and policy-implementation processes.[10] The main ones are legality, political acceptability, robustness under conditions of administrative implementation, and improvability.

Legality. A feasible policy must not violate constitutional, statutory, or common law rights. However, remember that legal rights are constantly changing and are often ambiguous. It is sometimes worth taking a gamble on a policy that might—or might not—be adjudged illegal when tested in court. (In such cases, advice of counsel is clearly in order to help craft the policy so that its survival chances are enhanced).

Note, however, that rights alleged to be natural or human are conceptually quite different from legal rights, despite the semantic similarity. Examples are abortion rights or right to life or a woman's right to her own body. Alleged natural or human "rights" are sometimes controversial in that some people would like to have them recognized as rights while others would oppose such recognition.

Political acceptability. A feasible policy must be politically acceptable, or at least not unacceptable. Political unacceptability is a combination of two things: too much opposition (which may be wide or intense or both) and/or too little support (which may be insufficiently broad or insufficiently intense or both).

Do not take a static view of unacceptability, however. Always ask yourself the question "If my favorite policy solution doesn't look acceptable under current conditions, what would it take to change those conditions?" You might discover that creative political strategizing can open up options that haven't been seriously considered before.

In assessing strategic limitations and possibilities, it will help to make use of various models of the political process. As I observed above, models are based on metaphors, and the ones that are likely to be most valuable in this case are these:

---

10. I said above that criteria apply to outcomes and not to alternatives. However, this statement needs a slight amendment in the case of practical criteria. These criteria apply not to outcomes but to the *prospects* an alternative faces as it goes through the policy adoption and implementation process.

- A complex game in which well-organized and well-positioned minorities enjoy special advantages
- A theater, in which the actors are elected officials who strive, with or without a basis in reality, to create a good appearance—to themselves, to each other, to the critics, and to the audience (whose approval, ultimately, is all-important)
- A marketplace of slogans, symbols, and ideas, with a mix of honorable merchants and hucksters as sellers and a mix of sophisticates and innocents as buyers
- A school in which elected officials learn how to do good policy design work and sometimes share their results and their methods with their classmates.

How exactly is one to "make use" of such models? Think of them as conceptual lenses. Observe the relevant political process through each of them in turn, and identify the probable pitfalls and opportunities brought into focus by each.[11]

Robustness and improvability. Policy ideas that sound great in theory often fail under conditions of actual field implementation. The implementation process has a life of its own. It is acted out through large and inflexible administrative systems and is distorted by bureaucratic interests. Policies that emerge in practice can diverge, even substantially, from policies as designed and adopted. A policy alternative, therefore, should be robust enough so that even if the implementation process does not go very smoothly, the policy outcomes will still prove to be satisfactory.

Some adverse implementation outcomes usually worth worrying about are long delays; capture of program or policy benefits by a relatively undeserving and unintended constituency; excessive budgetary or administrative costs; scandal from fraud, waste, and abuse that undermines political support and embarrasses supporters; and administrative complexities that leave citizens (and program managers) uncertain as to what benefits are available or what regulations must be complied with.

Even the best policy planners cannot get all the details right at the design stage. They should therefore allow room for policy implementers to improve on the original design. The most common vehicle for such improvement is participation in the implementation process by individuals and groups whose expertise or point of view was not included in the design phase.

However, note that the openness that makes for improvability can also, by opening the door to hostile political interests, diminish robustness. Hence, a

---

11. An analogous procedure was first given prominence by Graham Allison, in *Essence of Decision: Explaining the Cuban Missile Crisis* (Boston: Little, Brown, 1971).

very careful evaluation of the current factual situation—personalities, institutional demands and incentives, political vulnerabilities and so on—is usually in order.

In estimating robustness and improvability, models of bureaucracy can serve as useful conceptual lenses, as suggested above with regard to carrying out political analysis. I find the most useful metaphors about bureaucracy to be these, listed in no particular order:

- An automaton enacting preprogrammed routines ("standard operating procedures," or "SOPs")
- A person in an environment, driven by a will to survival, self-enhancement, and, under some conditions, self-actualization
- A political arena where individuals and factions jockey for influence over the organization's mission, access to its decision systems, and its prerequisites
- A tribe with its own rituals and an array of safeguards against contamination by "outsiders"
- A society of individuals cooperating towards a more-or-less common set of goals—though with various frictions and misunderstandings and some explicit and implicit bargaining over terms
- A structure of roles and interrelationships that are intended to complement one another in a rational division of labor
- An instrument used by "society" for "society's" own objectives.

Criteria in Optimization Models

Criteria such as efficiency, equity, political acceptability, and robustness are substantive. But we can think of criteria of a purely formal sort as well. For instance, we can distinguish between criterion values that we wish to *maximize,* those that must be *minimally satisfied,* and those for which "*more is better.*"

It is helpful to focus initially on one primary criterion, a *principal objective to be maximized* (or minimized). Typically this principal objective will be the obverse side of your problem definition. For instance, if your problem is too many homeless families, then your principal objective would probably be to minimize the number of homeless families. If the problem is that the greenhouse effect is growing too rapidly, a good statement of a principal objective might be "Minimize growth of the greenhouse effect." Naturally, there are other criteria to judge outcomes by, such as costliness, political acceptability, and economic justice. These should all enter into the final evaluation. However, it is very likely that unless you focus—initially, at least—on a single primary criterion and array others around it, you will find yourself getting very confused. As you get deeper into the analysis, and feel more comfortable with a multiplicity of important objectives, you may wish to drop your emphasis on a primary criterion and work on a more complex *objective function,* in the language of mathematical programming.

Linear programming. A mathematical (and now computer-accessible) technique for optimizing choice when you have a principal objective or an objective function and a scarce stock of resources for maximizing it is called *linear programming.*[12] Often, at least some of the resources (e.g., the agency budget and the available physical facilities promised by a nonprofit agency) are constrained. Even if the problem is not subject to simple quantitative assessment, analysts often find it useful to take advantage of the logical structure of linear programming to conceptualize their task. The conventional formulation then sounds like this: Maximize this objective (or objective function) subject to such-and-such resource constraints.

Here is an example from the homelessness problem: "Maximize the number of homeless individuals housed on any given night; subject to the constraints of $50,000 per night total budgetary cost to Agency X and to not putting shelters into Neighborhoods A and B for political reasons, and trying to give 'more' choice to the beneficiary population as to where they will take shelter."

Improving linguistic clarity. If it is possible to sort your criteria into those that refer to values to be maximized, values that stand as constraints, and values that have a more-is-better quality, keep the different statuses of the criteria in mind. Be conscious of them. You can do this with a simple verbal trick: As appropriate, define your criteria as "Maximize such-and-such value"; "Satisfy such-and-such value constraint"; and "Get more of such-and-such value."

5. Project the Outcomes

Now, for each of the alternatives on your current list, project all the outcomes (or impacts) that you or other interested parties might reasonably care about.

This is the hardest step in the Eightfold Path. Even veteran policy analysts do not usually do it very well. Not surprisingly, analysts often duck it entirely, disguising their omission by a variety of subterfuges. Hence, the most important advice about this step is simple: Do it.

There are (at least) three great practical as well as psychological difficulties. First, "policy" is about the future, not about the past or the present, but we can never really be certain about how the future will unfold, not even if we engage it with the best of intentions and the most thoughtful of policy designs. Second,

---

12. See Stokey and Zeckhauser, *A Primer,* chap. 11.

"Project the outcomes" is another way of saying, "Be realistic." Yet, realism is often uncomfortable. Most people prefer optimism. Policy can actually affect people's lives, fortunes, and sacred honor, for better or for worse. Making policy, therefore, imposes a moral burden that is heavier than many people care to acknowledge. Understandably, we would rather believe that our preferred or recommended policy alternative will actually accomplish what we hope and that it will impose fewer costs than we might realistically fear. Thirdly, there is what is sometimes called "the 51-49 principle." That is, in the thick of the policy fray, we are driven out of pure self-defense to treat 51 percent confidence in our projection as though it deserved 100 percent confidence, with the result that we sometimes mislead not only others but ourselves as well. The first difficulty—namely, that we can never have wholly convincing evidence about the future—compounds the second and third, inasmuch as our wishful thinking is not readily disciplined by reference to empirical demonstrations and proofs.

These cautionary notes notwithstanding, remember that we do not wish to swing toward pessimism either. Realistic projection is our goal.

Projection = Model + Evidence

In this section I discuss, in a very general way, the logic of combining models and evidence to produce useable projections of policy outcomes attached to the various alternatives being considered. The logic is largely that of common sense, but with some important additions.

The first addition is that of metaphor. Policy analysis, as we have seen, makes use of the metaphors behind the models—metaphors such as "bureaucracy as automation" and "politics as theater" and "this piece of the world as production system"—to yield qualitative insights about important causal relationships. The especially important relationships are those that might afford useful intervention points in complex systems and that present potential pitfalls in policy adoption or implementation processes.

Second, policy analysis uses social science to the degree that it can. A great deal of social science is directed towards answering the question "Is Model X of this piece of the world realistic?" Social scientific studies of this type can often be useful for diagnosing the existence of problems, mapping trends, and deciding whether some seemingly smart practice (see Part III) is worth trying to replicate. You should be careful, however, to avoid using the social scientific standard of adequacy for judgments about the realism of a model, which are quite conservative. In policy analysis the looser, but more appropriate, standard should be whether reliance on a model can lead to better results and avoid worse results, than less disciplined guesswork.

Third, policy analysis, as we have seen, uses multiple models. Most social science, in imitation of the hard sciences, looks for "the best" model (and, for some practitioners, "the true" model). Because all models abstract from reality, however, even the best models are never complete. While such abstraction can advance the progress of science, in the world of policy, where real consequences of policy choices are to be experienced by real people, no facet of a problem or the possible alternatives to be adopted can be exempted from analysis. Whatever models *can* be employed to illuminate some important facet of the problem or of the possible outcomes *should* be employed—even if doing so results in an inelegant and ad hoc multiplication of subanalyses.

When it comes to employing multiple models, common sense, unfortunately, is no more enthusiastic than social science. The public debate over whether, or how, to attack Microsoft's dominance in computer software, for instance, features the company as either a monopolistic rent-seeker or a powerful innovator and promoter of standardization, whereas it is clearly all these at the same time.

Finally, even when you have embarked on using adequately realistic models of sufficient number and variety, they still need to be used in conjunction with evidence about "initial conditions," or the facts on the ground as they currently exist. Although the projections of many models are not particularly sensitive to initial conditions, some are. These are the models that bear on projections of political acceptability and on the robustness of an alternative to the stresses of the implementation process.

Attach Magnitude Estimates

Projecting outcomes often requires you to think not just about the general direction of an outcome but about the magnitude as well. Typically it's not enough to say, "We expect this program to have a very positive effect on reducing unwanted teenage pregnancies." Instead, you'd want to say, "We expect this program to reduce by one-hundred to three-hundred the number of unwanted teenage pregnancies per year in this community over the next five years."

Sometimes a point estimate of your single best guess about some magnitude will suffice. But in some cases you should provide a range.

Break-Even Estimates

A convenient way to handle uncertainty in estimation is with *break-even estimations*. These use what you do know or can reasonably assume in order to *frame the residual uncertainty* in a way that is meaningful for decision making. Break-even analysis takes advantage of the binary accept-or-reject logical framework that decision makers generally use. It is this framework that helps structure the estimation of residual uncertainties.

Suppose, for instance, that some youth-guidance-oriented policy meant to reduce incarceration of juveniles is under consideration and has known costs of $1 million, but the level of effectiveness is speculative. You build a frame for the remaining uncertainty in four steps:

1. Locate the point of minimum acceptable effectiveness given the costs. Ask, "What is the minimum level of effectiveness this policy would have to achieve in order to justify our spending $1 million?" Your answer: "Different observers have different opinions about how much avoiding an incarceration is worth, but leaving that aside and going with my own values, I'd say that three-hundred a year, or a 15 percent reduction, is the minimum I would accept given the expenditure of $1 million."[13]

2. Referring back to your model of the processes that create the problem and hold it in place, ask, "What new processes, or changes in old ones, could conceivably produce this level of effectiveness?" This is largely a qualitative analysis. The answer might be "Based on previous documentation of how the guidance process works, we can safely say that it works in different ways with different sorts of kids—when it works at all, that is. It can provide about half the kids more constructive life choices; in about a quarter of the cases it works through heightening the (realistic) perception of punishment; and in about a quarter of cases we are just crossing our fingers."

3. You estimate how likely (or unlikely) it is that the processes for improvement thus identified will actually produce the required—that is, the break-even—level of effectiveness. It is particularly helpful to ask whether the break-even level (15 percent in this case) looks like a plausible number given what is known or assumed about the effectiveness in similar circumstances of similar sorts of interventions. If the number is implausibly high, you might then go on to ask whether special circumstances of some sort might be at work in this case to help achieve it. Note that in this and the previous step you must rely on what we might think of as "theory," or self-conscious and evidence-based reasoning about the way causal processes work. Typically, these are the weakest links in the chain of policy-analytic reasoning. That is why it is particularly important—and

---

13. Some people speak of *switchpoint analysis* and would refer to the 15 percent here as the switchpoint at which a decision maker would switch from a favorable view of this policy to an unfavorable view or vice versa. Others refer to *threshold analysis* and would call the 15 percent figure the threshold level of effectiveness we would need to assume in order to justify choosing this alternative.

particularly difficult—to take this step as thoughtfully, self-critically, and responsibly as possible.

4. Estimate the probability of failure and the political and other costs of having to accept failure—asking yourself whether they would be tolerable should they be incurred.

Here are two more examples:

- Policy X for establishing a chain of wildlife refuges looks like an excellent choice to implement a broader conservation agenda, provided the funding really comes through as planned. But it might not, because federal grant-in-aid resources might not be forthcoming, or the governor might give the policy lower priority than she now promises, or some development interests that have their eye on two of the designated sites might find a way to block it. You interview your client, a state environmental agency director, and determine that she likes the program so much that she is willing to go for it if it has at least a 50-50 chance of working out. Your analysis can then focus her attention on why, after considerable research, you have concluded that it has a somewhat better (or somewhat worse) chance than 50-50, even though you would find it impossible to specify exactly how much better (or worse).

- Building a new stadium for the Hometown Heroes looks like a good idea, given the nature of the costs and benefits, if average daily attendance turns out to be no less than 10,000. That's the break-even attendance figure for you and the relevant decision makers. Then it's up to them to decide (1) how confident they are that this break-even level will be reached and (2) whether that degree of confidence is enough to warrant making an affirmative decision. You would then organize your presentation of facts and opinions so that it focuses on these two key issues.[14]

Here is a semantic suggestion for making use of the logic of break-even analysis. Assuming for the moment that benefits are uncertain while costs are not, ask yourself these two questions: (1) "Given what I know for sure about the

---

14. A special case of break-even estimation is a fortiori estimation. If you hypothesize worst-case estimates of all important parameters that are still uncertain and the policy alternative still satisfies your decision criterion, the alternative will, a fortiori, prove satisfactory even if more careful estimates were to be more favorable. In that case, the more careful estimates are unnecessary. See MacRae and Whittington, *Expert Advice,* 218–19, on a fortiori analysis and, more generally, 209–24 on the question of precision versus approximation in projecting outcomes.

costs of this alternative, what is the minimum help we need to get from Condition X to ensure adequately offsetting benefits?" and (2) "How reasonable is it to believe that Condition X will actually produce that minimum?" Question 1 can also be framed in terms of known benefits and the conditions that would yield minimally acceptable costs.

The Optimism Problem

Great ventures require optimism. Because even small ventures by government can affect so many lives, they are in their own way "great." Hence, a little optimism is beneficial. But how do you guard against excessive optimism?

Scenario writing. What scenarios might cause the proposal to fail to produce the desired outcome (e.g., solving or sufficiently mitigating the policy problems)? Do not create such scenarios from whole cloth. Be realistic. And yet, let your imagination run a little, so that you have a good chance of thinking of the most dangerous possibilities. In particular, think about the dangers of the implementation process, political and otherwise. Scenario writing also benefits from thinking about possible failures from a vantage point in the future looking backward. For instance:

- In a health or safety regulatory program, the scientific or technical knowledge necessary to produce rational and legally defensible standards might prove to be lacking. As a result, five years from now, symbolic politics, corruption, industry capture, or excessive regulatory zeal will have filled the vacuum.
- Time passes, and budgetary resources and political support that were once available slip away under the impact of electoral change and changes in the economy. The program, begun under nurturant leaders and accompanied by editorialists' applause, becomes consolidated with another program, will have been taken over by a different bureaucratic unit, and eventually disappears.
- A successful state program designed to furnish technical assistance to extremely poor rural counties will have added a mandate to aid many not-so-poor urban counties, with the result that scarce program resources will have been dissipated and squandered.[15]
- A program that subsidizes research and development of "fish protein concentrate," intended as a cheap and nutritious food additive, is launched with great fanfare. Five years from now it will prove to have been stalled,

---

15. I call this scenario *piling on*. See Eugene Bardach, *The Implementation Game: What Happens after a Bill Becomes a Law* (Cambridge, Mass.: MIT Press, 1977).

permanently, by the Food and Drug Administration, which will not have been able to assimilate this product into its standard operating procedures for regulatory review.

Notice that these scenarios are written in the future perfect tense. This encourages concreteness, which is a helpful stimulant to the imagination.[16] It often helps your scenario-writing to start with a list of adverse implementation outcomes and to conjure up one or more scenarios about how each of these might occur. Remember the list above of such outcomes: long delays; "capture" of program or policy benefits by a relatively undeserving and unintended constituency; excessive budgetary or administrative costs; scandal from fraud, waste, and abuse that undermines political support and embarrasses supporters; and administrative complexities that leave citizens (and program managers) uncertain as to what benefits are available or what regulations must be complied with.

The other-guy's-shoes heuristic. Imagine yourself in the other guy's shoes. Say to yourself, "If I were X, how would I act?" And then proceed to crawl into X's mind and play out, in your own mind, what X might do. Do this systematically for each of the important stakeholders or other affected parties. The value of doing this is that you will discover them to be adapting in surprising ways to the new policy situation you might be creating, and with results that might cause trouble for your policy design.

For example, under chemical right-to-know laws, workers have the right to know what substances they have been exposed to, and they may examine health records maintained by employers. If you were a worker, how might you use this law? Might you use the information to quit your present job? Demand a higher wage? Demand protective equipment? Sue your employer? Put pressure on your union representatives?

And how would your union representative react to such pressure? Might this pressure make the representative's job harder—or perhaps easier in some way?

Now, suppose you were an employer. Given what you expect your workers might do, you would face incentives to make adaptations or countermoves. Might you stop keeping all health records not explicitly required by law? Might you continue keeping records but permit doctors to perform only selected lab tests? And if you were a worker and saw your employer doing these things, what countermoves would you make?

Not all the moves and countermoves of players wearing the other guy's shoes will necessarily lead to trouble for the policy alternative you are evaluating. Many such adaptation sequences may prove to be helpful, in the sense that they may

---

16. For more details, see Karl E. Weick, *The Social Psychology of Organizing*, 2d ed. (Reading, Mass.: Addison-Wesley, 1979), 195–200.

help society adjust to the changes set in motion by the new policy. At some point in the 1970s the Federal Trade Commission (FTC) attacked the problem of retailers' evading implied warranty obligations for defective products by selling installment debts to banks and other collectors that had no duty, under the so-called holder-in-due-course doctrine, to fix the product or to refrain from collecting on the installment debt. The FTC solution was, in effect, to abolish the protections of the holder-in-due-course doctrine. Banks complained that they did not want to go into the toaster repair business. But if you put yourself in the shoes of a bank manager suddenly obliged to become a toaster repairer, might you not have thought of contracting out your repair obligations to repair specialists, or perhaps arranging, for example, not to buy installment debts from retailers who you believed could not be relied upon to make good on their implied warranties?

Undesirable side effects. Analysts are often cautioned to think about *unanticipated consequences.* But this term is not appropriate, for it is often used to refer to perfectly anticipatable, though undesirable, side effects. Here are some common undesirable but anticipatable side effects in public programs:

- *Moral hazard* increases. That is, your policy has the effect of insulating people from the consequences of their actions. For example, increasing the size of unemployment benefits has the side effect of blunting the incentives to search for a replacement job.

- *Overregulation in the health and safety areas.* One possible adverse result of setting health or safety standards "too high" and enforcing them "too uniformly" is that you increase private sector costs beyond some desirable optimum. For instance, given most people's private preferences for safety, imposing auto bumper standards that cost some $25 per vehicle but that have only trivial effects on improving vehicle crashworthiness would not pass a conventional benefit-cost test. A second adverse result might be that you inadvertently cause a shift away from the regulated activity into some other activity that—perversely—is less safe or less healthful. For instance, some observers argue that overregulating the safety features of nuclear power production has caused a shift toward coal, which they argue is much more hazardous than nuclear power.

- *Rent seekers*—that is, interests looking out for profitable niches protected from full competition—distort the program to serve their own interests. It is not inevitable that suppliers of goods and services to the government, including civil servants, will find ways to capture "rents." But it often happens (e.g., with many defense contractors). Rent seeking also occurs in less obvious ways (e.g., when some regulated firms successfully lobby for regulations that impose much higher compliance costs on their competitors than on themselves).

The ethical costs of optimism. It is hard to overstate the importance of worrying about the possible adverse side effects of otherwise "good" policies, not to mention the possibility that even intended "good" main effects may fail to materialize under many circumstances.[17] The ethical policy analyst always poses the question, "If people actually were to follow my advice, what might be the costs of my having been wrong, and who would have to bear them?" And keep in mind that the analyst typically is *not* one of the parties who have to bear the costs of his or her mistakes.

The Outcomes Matrix

The step of projecting outcomes leads you into a dense thicket of information. You will not want to present or discuss all of it in your final report. But at any point along the way you might need to be able to stand back and assess complex and uncertain scenarios for up to eight or ten basic alternatives combined with their principal variants. A convenient way to get an overview of all this information is to display it in an outcomes matrix. A smaller version of such a matrix might also prove useful in your final report.

The typical outcome matrix format arrays your policy alternatives down the rows and your evaluative criteria across the columns. Any cell, then, contains the projected outcome of the row alternative as assessed by reference to the column criterion. Table I.I (p. 36) is an example I created a few years ago in order to compare projected outcomes for three alternative systems to periodically inspect California's 10 million automobiles for smog control compliance. In this example, Baker, Smith, and Jones, analysts working for three different government agencies and with somewhat opposed policy views, are making rather different projections of outcomes for each of these alternatives. I record their rival projections in the cells where they differed.

The smog check system involved biennial inspection at the time of vehicle reregistration in any one of several thousand approved service stations. IM 240 would have required biennial inspection using more sophisticated testing machinery at any one of many fewer centralized and specialized testing facilities. Remote sensing was an emerging technology that would simply monitor cars from roadside vans and initiate enforcement measures against those determined to be out of compliance.[18]

If you cannot fill in the cell with a quantitatively expressed description of

---

17. See the Behn and Vaupel chapter on "Assessing Your Ignorance" in *Quick Analysis*.
18. For other examples, see Tables 9–4, 9–5, 9–8, and 9–9 in Stokey and Zeckhauser, *A Primer*. See also the discussion in Weimer and Vining, *Policy Analysis*, 282–89, and their sample matrices on 285–313.

TABLE I.I. **OUTCOMES PROJECTED BY THREE DIFFERENT ANALYSTS FOR THREE ALTERNATIVE FLEET INSPECTION SYSTEMS**

	Criteria			
Alternatives	Come closer to needed cleanup (percentage attained)	Minimize cost per ton of pollution reduced ($)	Minimize consumer time (minutes)	Reduce test cost to vehicle owner ($)
IM 240	Baker: 100 Smith: 0	Baker: <SC* Smith: Millions	Jones: 60 Smith: >60	Jones: <SC* Baker: >SC*
Modified smog check	Baker: 50 Smith: 0	Baker: Thousands Smith: Millions	Jones: 75 Smith: 75	Smith: 35
Remote sensing	Baker: 0 Smith: 100	Baker: Millions Smith: 200	Consensus: 0 for most drivers	Consensus: 0 for most owners

SC = smog check.

the projected outcome, you might settle for a verbal descriptor like "very good" or a symbolic descriptor like + or −.

Linguistic Pitfalls

A common error that occurs in labeling the criteria columns in such a matrix is to fail to indicate what *value* is at stake and in what dimensions the measurement is being done. For instance, if you are assessing a rental subsidy program, and you enter a plus sign in a column labeled "Landlord/tenant relations," the reader may not know whether you think relations will become more harmonious, more confrontational, less dominated by landlords, less dominated by tenants, or something else. It is not sufficient that your surrounding text makes your intention clear; the matrix label itself must be informative. In my illustrative matrix I did not simply write *cleanup* or *cost* or *time*. Within the space constraints I tried to indicate the metric and the desired direction in which it should move. In many cases it helps to insert *maximize* or *minimize* in the criterion label.

You can simplify the mass of information you need to display and assimilate in your outcome matrix or in any other form if you eliminate information about outcomes that will be the same for all the alternatives. This omission is particularly useful if the outcomes that all the alternatives will produce are ambiguous or uncertain: you will be spared the trouble of having to make the difficult projections involved.

6. Confront the Trade-offs

It sometimes happens that one of the policy alternatives under consideration is expected to produce a better outcome than any of the other alternatives with regard to every single evaluative criterion. In that case there are no trade-offs among the alternatives. This is called *dominance.* Usually, though, you are less fortunate, and you must clarify the trade-offs between outcomes associated with different policy options for the sake of your client and/or audience.

The most common trade-off is between money and a good or service received by some proportion of the citizenry, such as extending library hours from 8 P.M. till 10 P.M. weighed against a cost of $200,000 annually. Another common trade-off, especially in regulatory policies, involves weighing privately borne costs (a company's installing pollution abatement equipment) against social benefits (improved health and the protection of forests).

As economics teaches us, trade-offs occur at the margin. Trade-off analysis tells us something like this: If we spend an extra X dollars for an extra unit of Service Y, we can get an extra Z units of good outcome. This kind of analysis puts the decision maker in the position to answer the question "Does society (or do you) value Z more or less than X?" and then to follow the obvious implication of the answer ("If yes, decide for another Y; if no, don't").

A linguistic device to help you keep focused on the margin is frequent use of the word *extra.* Note that this word appears three times in the example analysis in the preceding paragraph.

Some units of Service Y can be purchased only in "lumps" larger than one—sometimes much larger. Consider transportation services provided by highways and bridges. Y might be one passenger trip from A to B, but most transportation construction projects (highway enlargements, new bridge crossings) can be undertaken only for minimum bundles of Y that run into the thousands of trips. Or suppose that a police chief must choose one of two "lumpy" alternatives, such as $1 million per year for more overtime on the night shift or $250,000 (annualized) for more rapid replacement of police cars. The first alternative is lumpy because the police union insists on a minimum overtime rate for all 150 officers on the shift, and the second is lumpy because the auto supplier charges much less per vehicle after some threshold number of vehicles. If, say, the projected decrease in burglaries from increased overtime were 200 per year and that from newer vehicles were 50, the trade-off confronting the decision maker at the margin is an extra $5,000 per extra burglary prevented. In this case the "margin" is a lumpy

150 burglaries and $750,000. (Criteria other than burglary prevention and cost efficiency would, of course, be relevant to this problem.)

Commensurability

Suppose some Alternative A_1 stacks up very well on Criterion C_1, moderately well on C_2, and poorly on C_3. And suppose that A_2 stacks up in the opposite way. We can choose between the two alternatives only if we can weight the importance of the criteria and if we can express their relative weights in units that are commensurable across the criteria. As you may have heard, money as the commensurable metric is everybody's favorite candidate. Using money as the metric is a very good idea, and it often works much better than one might imagine. For instance, even the "value of life" can sometimes be reasonably well described in the metric "willingness to pay X dollars for a reduction in the risk of death by Y percent a year" or something like it.

However, there are limits to the money metric and to commensurability as well. In order to reach a summary judgment as to how much political equality to give up in a political redistricting case, for instance, in exchange for how much more African-American voter power, it seems impossible even to state the trade-off in meaningful terms. In general, this problem is known as *the multiattribute problem*. In some deep sense it is logically insoluble, although some heuristics are available to help trim it down to its minimally irreducible size.[19]

Break-even analysis revisited. We have seen how break-even analysis can help you (1) focus on which residual uncertainties you have to estimate and (2) frame the terms in which that estimate must be given ("We have to believe Alternative A_1 will produce at least X results in order to justify choosing it"). We turn now to how break-even analysis can also help solve commensurability problems.

Consider those policy areas, such as safety regulation, where we are often implicitly trading off dollars against risks to life. It might be supposed that in order to assess these proposals you would have to "decide what a human life is really worth"— a task many of us, quite understandably, are unwilling to perform. The task is made somewhat more tractable, however, if you work with quantitative estimates and apply break-even analysis. Suppose, for instance, you are considering

---

19. Stokey and Zeckhauser, *A Primer,* 117–33. See also MacRae and Whittington, *Expert Advice,* 201–3. One potentially misleading heuristic has the analyst creating a score for each alternative with respect to each criterion and then manipulating the scores arithmetically. It is easy to get the arithmetic right, but it is often hard to come up with scoring procedures that are not at some level arbitrary (e.g., anchored against some arbitrarily defined level of excellence or its opposite).

whether or not to impose a new auto design standard on the industry that will improve safety and save an estimated twenty-five lives per year every year into the indefinite future. The cost of meeting the standard is estimated at $50 million every year indefinitely. The trade-off at the margin appears to be, therefore, "$2 million per life." But you don't have to answer the question "What's a human life *really worth?*" in order to make at least some sense of this decision. You do have to answer the question, "Is a statistical life (that is, the life of an unknown individual 'drawn' in a random manner from some population, rather than a named person's life) worth at least $2 million?" That is a break-even analysis sort of question. For reasons best known to yourself, it may be obvious to you that a statistical life surely is—or isn't. And while it's very difficult to decide whether the worth of a statistical life falls on one or the other side of some monetary boundary, it's a lot less difficult than coming up with a point value.

Even this sort of trade-off calculation is troubling to many people, and some find it morally repugnant. Unfortunately, repugnant or not, it is in a sense inevitable. Whatever position you take on the auto safety design standard described, you are by implication also taking a position on the dollars/risk-to-life trade-off: if you favor the standard, you implicitly believe the trade-off is worthwhile, whereas if you oppose it, you don't. Fortunately, this logical implication has its uses. You may in many circumstances quite sensibly prefer to rely on your "intuition" rather than on some complicated systematic method. Once you have reached your conclusion based on intuition, though, you can *check* your intuition by asking yourself, "Since the implication of my policy choice is that I value X as being worth at least (or at most) thus-and-such, do I really believe that?"

Without Projecting Outcomes, There's Nothing to Trade Off

A common pitfall in confronting trade-offs is to think and speak of the trade-offs as being across *alternatives* rather than across projected *outcomes* (e.g., "trading off twenty foot-patrol police officers in the late night hours against a lower-maintenance-cost fleet of police vehicles"). Although there is such a trade-off, you'll see, with a second's thought, that you can't do anything at all with it. Both alternatives must first be converted into outcomes before genuine trade-offs can be confronted. Thus, the competing outcomes might be fifty (plus or minus . . .) burglaries per year prevented by the police versus a savings of $300,000 in fleet maintenance.

Simplify the Comparison Process

Do what you can to simplify the process of comparing alternatives and focusing on the critical tradeoffs.

Eliminate. First, eliminate any alternative that is clearly dominated by at least one other alternative. Secondly, look for alternatives that *would* be dominated if you weighted one criterion (or more) rather less heavily than most of the other criteria. Upon reflection, you might decide that this criterion (and possibly others as well) *should* be weighted this low, and that these alternatives too can be dropped from further consideration.

Pay special attention to the alternative of simply letting present trends continue. If it has not been dropped by this point in the analysis, now is the time to check if it is sufficiently dominated by other alternatives to justify discarding it.

Compare to a base case. Even if you drop "letting present trends continue" as a reasonable alternative, you might still want to retain the *set of outcomes* that you project for it as a *benchmark* against which to compare other sets of projected outcomes. Such a benchmark set is often called a *base case*. Using a base case as a benchmark is helpful almost apart from what it is. You may wish to use other projections as base cases besides—or in addition to—"letting present trends continue." Other possibly illuminating base cases are:

> "The likely outcome if we don't manage to head off what the Governor's office [or some other powerful faction] is planning . . ."

> "Our ideal set of outcomes if political conditions were just a bit more favorable . . ."

> "The worst-case scenario which we have to prevent practically at any cost . . ."

If you decide to use a base case as a benchmark, you should probably *make another outcomes* matrix in which each cell entry appraises the projected outcome against its projected base case counterpart. Of course, you may wish to construct your original outcomes matrix in this fashion to begin with.

7. Decide!

The "Decide!" step appears in the Eightfold Path as a check on how well you have done your work up to this point. Even though you personally may not be the decision maker, you should at this point pretend that you are. Then, decide what to do based on your own analysis. If you find this decision difficult or troublesome, perhaps the reason is that you have not clarified the trade-offs sufficiently, or that you have not said quite enough about the probability of serious implementation problems emerging (or not emerging), or that a crucial cost estimate is still too fuzzy and uncertain, or that you have not approximated carefully enough the elasticity of some important demand curve, and so on.

Think of it this way: Unless you can convince *yourself* of the plausibility of some course of action, you probably won't be able to convince your client—and rightly so.

Of course, when you tell your story to your client or any other audience, you might not think it appropriate to make reference to your own decision. You might, instead, simply limit your story to a clarification of the relevant trade-offs and leave the decision completely up to the audience.

The Twenty-Dollar-Bill Test

You should at this point subject your favored policy alternative to *the twenty-dollar bill test*. The name of the test is based on an old joke making fun of economists. Two friends are walking down the street when one stops to pick something up. "What about that—a twenty-dollar bill!" he says. "Couldn't be," says the other, an economist. "If it were, somebody would have picked it up already." The analogy is this: *If your favorite policy alternative is such a great idea, how come it's not happening already?* The most common sources of failure on this test are neglecting to consider the resistance of bureaucratic and other stakeholders in the status quo, and the lack of an entrepreneur in the relevant policy environment who has the incentives to pick up what seems like a great idea and see it through. Failure on this test is not fatal, of course. Just keep fiddling till you invent a variant of your basic idea that will pass.

8. Tell Your Story

After many iterations of all the above steps—redefining your problem, reconceptualizing your alternatives, reconsidering your criteria, reassessing your projections, reevaluating the trade-offs—you are ready to tell your story to some audience. The audience might be your client, or it might be broader. It might be hostile, or it might be friendly.

The New York Taxi Driver Test

Before proceeding further, you need a little reality check. Suppose you have just caught a cab in New York City. While you are stalled in traffic, the cabbie asks you about your work. You say you are a "policy analyst working for . . ." He says, "What's that?" You explain that you've been working on "the problem of . . ." He says, "So, what's the answer?" You have one minute to offer a coherent, down-to-earth explanation before he starts accusing you of being a pointy-headed intellectual or worse. If you feel yourself starting to hem and haw, you haven't really understood your own conclusions at a deep enough level to make sense to others, and probably not to yourself either. Back to the drawing board until you get it straight.

Now consider the possibility that someone might actually wish to base a real decision or a policy proposal on your analysis. (It's been known to happen.) Even if you, as an analyst, would not have to deal directly with such a tough audience as the New York taxi driver and his kindred, it's likely that someone will have to do so. At the very least, therefore, you'll have to be able to explain your basic story to someone in sufficiently simple and down-to-earth terms that that someone will be able to carry on with the task of public, democratic education.

You, Your Client, and Your Audiences

Assuming you've passed the New York taxi driver test, identify and assess the likely non-taxi-driver audience(s).

First comes your client, the person or persons whose approval you need most—your hierarchical superior(s), perhaps, or those who are funding your work. What is the relationship between your and your client? What you say and how you say it should depend a great deal on whether your relationship is long-term and on whether it is carried on face-to-face. In particular, how easy will it be for you to correct any misunderstandings that might arise?

Next, think about the larger political environment. Who do you think will "use" the analysis and for what purpose(s)? Will anyone pick up your results for use in an advocacy context? Would you regard this use of your results as desirable? Desirable if certain advocates use your work and undesirable if others do so? Do you want to do anything to "segregate" your policy advice by the type of audience you might want it to reach—or not to reach? Are you, perhaps inadvertently, using scare words that will alienate certain audiences?

If you are making a clear recommendation, make sure you raise and rebut possible objections to it that various important audiences might think of. Also make sure that you compare it to what you or others might regard as the next best course of action, to show why yours is better.

What Medium to Use?

You can tell your story in written or in oral form. In either case, communicate simply and clearly. The guiding principle is that other things being equal, shorter is always better. In written presentations, good subheadings and graphics can make reading and comprehension easier. Visual aids such as flip charts, overhead transparencies, and computer-based slide projections often help in oral presentations.

Oral presentations require practice, self-discipline, and a little knowledge of some basic principles. The most basic of the basic principles are to speak *very slowly and distinctly;* to speak loudly enough to be heard throughout the room, even over distracting noises; to speak in a lower register, which tends to increase perceived trustworthiness and credibility; not to fidget but not to stand like a stick either; to make lots of eye contact with audience members; and in doing so not to favor one side of the room over another. Speaking slowly and distinctly is probably harder than you think—and more important, too.

Your Story Should Have a Logical Narrative Flow

Your story's flow should be designed with the reader's (or listener's) needs and interests and abilities in mind. In both written and oral presentations, it should be evident to the audience what motivates the entire analysis. Therefore it is best to open with a statement of the problem your analysis addresses.[20]

It is also important to motivate the more detailed steps in the flow of the analysis, that is, the sections, paragraphs, and sentences. Most readers will look for the motivation of any element in what immediately precedes it. Therefore, avoid lengthy digressions. For these reasons, be wary of sections you are tempted to label "Background." Similarly, the phrase "Before turning to . . ." is usually a sign of undigested material. Many readers will be alert to the danger signs; therefore you should be, too. The same holds for "It is first necessary to explain/ understand the history of . . ." Policy analysis, remember, is about the future. Perhaps surprisingly, it is often not obvious how, or whether, history affects the future. It might do so, but the burden should be on the writer or speaker to show exactly how this effect will come about.

A common, though not uniformly applicable, organizing framework is to begin with a good problem definition and then to treat each alternative you consider as a major section. Within each such section, you would project the probable outcome(s) of implementing the alternative and assess how likely such outcome(s) are in the light of some causal model and associated evidence. Following these discussions, you might review and summarize the alternative outcomes and discuss their trade-offs. Note that in this framework there is no special discussion of criteria. However, sometimes an explicit discussion of criteria is

---

20. An unusually fine manual on how to give slide-based oral briefings is published by the RAND Corporation, *Guidelines for Preparing RAND Briefings* (Santa Monica, Calif.: RAND Corporation, 1994), publication no. CP(I)-269.

important; it might appear either just before or just after the presentation of the alternatives and their associated outcomes.

Some Common Pitfalls

Following the Eightfold Path. Sometimes it helps to structure your narrative flow as though you were leading the reader by the hand down the Eightfold Path. But usually this approach is a mistake. The purpose of the Eightfold Path, remember, is to help you *think through* a complicated problem. It is not at all necessary to use it in telling the story, though some aspects of it sometimes help.

Compulsive qualifying. Don't interrupt the flow of an argument in order to display all the qualifications and uncertainties about some particular element in the argument. A way around this pitfall is to use adjectives or adjective phrases like *most, on average,* and *more often than not* to state the generality, and then to return to the exceptions in the next section. (Or if the exceptions and qualifications really can't wait, try a parenthesized sentence or a footnote.)

Showing your work. Don't include every fact you ever learned in the course of your research. Even if you've done a good and thorough job of research and analysis, most of what you learned will prove to be irrelevant by the time you've finished. That is, you will have succeeded in focusing your own attention on what's really important and in downplaying what only appeared important at the beginning. You don't usually need to take your reader on the same wandering course you were obliged to follow.

Listing without explaining. Should you list every alternative policy that you intend to analyze in the report before you actually get around to providing the analysis? Such a list is a good thing when the alternatives are not numerous, when they are all taken seriously either by you or by your audience, and when they will prepare the reader's mind for the detailed assessment that will follow. However, if you have many alternatives to consider, the reader will forget what's on the list, and if some of the alternatives turn out to be easily dismissed upon closer scrutiny, you'll simply have been setting up straw men and wasting the reader's mental energy.

Similarly, be cautious about listing every evaluative criterion of interest before coming to the assessment of the alternatives being considered. Usually—though not always—there is not much of interest to be said in a separate section about criteria that can't be better said when you're actually writing the assessment sections.

Style. Avoid the pomposity and circumlocutions of the bureaucratic and the academic styles. (Essential reading: George Orwell, *Politics and the English Language.*) Also to be avoided: a chatty style, and an insider's style (e.g., "We all understand what creeps our opponents are, don't we?").

Report Format

Unless the report is short, begin with an executive summary.

If the report is over fifteen to twenty pages, say, a table of contents is often helpful. If there are many tables and figures, either in the text or in the appendixes, a table of contents for these can be helpful. Detailed technical information or calculations should appear in appendixes rather than in the text. However, enough technical information, and reasoning, should appear in the text itself to persuade the reader that you really do know what you're talking about and that your argument is at least credible.

Use headings and subheadings to help keep the reader oriented and to break up large bodies of text; make sure your formatting (caps, italics, boldface, indentation) is compatible with, and indeed supports, the logical hierarchy of your argument.

Table format. Current professional practice is very poor with respect to the formatting of tables. Do not imitate it, but strive to improve it. Every table (or figure) should have a number (Table 1, for instance, or Figure 3.A) and a title. The title should be intelligible; it is often useful to have the title describe the main point to be learned from the table (e.g., "Actual Risks of Drinking and Driving Rise Rapidly with Number of Drinks—But Are Greatly Underestimated by College Students"). Each row and column in a table must be labeled, and the label should be interpretable without too much difficulty.

Tables normally either are purely descriptive or seek to demonstrate some causal relationship. Regarding the latter, it is usually desirable to create tables that make a single point (or at most two), and that can stand alone without need of much explanation in the text that surrounds them. It is usually better to use two or three small tables to make two or three points than to use one massive table and then to try to explain its contents by means of the surrounding text.

Tables usually require footnotes. There should almost always be a source note at the bottom of the table. The footnotes sometimes refer to data sources used to make the table and sometimes attempt to clarify the meaning of the row or column labels, which are necessarily abbreviated.

References and sources. Include page(s) listing references and sources at the end of the presentation. Books and articles should be cited in academic style (alphabetical order by author). The main point is to provide bibliographic help to curious and/or skeptical readers who want to track down references for themselves. There are several acceptable styles, though a good model is the one used in the book review section of the *Journal of Policy Analysis and Management,* which is simple and direct.

The current trend is toward "scientific citation" in lieu of footnote references in the text. That is, cite last name(s) of author(s) and year of publication in parentheses in text; the reader then checks the references section at the end for the full citation. If you follow this practice, the reference section should list the author(s) and the date *before* listing the title of the work and publication details. Sometimes you will want to include a page number in the parenthetical citation as well.

Legal citation style is quite different. If most of the references are legal, then it is advisable to move all references to bottom-of-page footnotes. However, you can keep the scientific citation format within the footnote.

Notes are easier to read if they appear on the same page as the referenced text, that is, if you display them as footnotes rather than as endnotes.

Memo Format:

[Date]

To: [Recipient name(s), official position(s)]

From: [Your name, position. Sign or initial next to or above your name.]

Subject: [Grammatically correct and brief description of the subject]

[First sentence or two should remind recipient of the fact that she or he asked you for a memo on this subject, and why. Alternatively, you could say why you are submitting this memo on this subject to the recipient at this time.]

[If memo is long, you might open and close with a summary paragraph or two. If you open with a long summary, the closing summary can be short.]

[If memo is long, consider breaking it up with subheads.]

The Sound Bite and the Press Release

Most policy analyses do not become the subject of a press release or a radio or TV sound bite. Some do, however. Others become candidates for such treatment, and all can profit, even in their extended form, by the analyst's reflecting on how to condense the essential message. Hence, it will probably serve an analytical purpose, and sometimes a political purpose, if you sketch out a press release and/ or a few ideas for sound bites. You might also wish to think strategically and defensively to see how an opponent might characterize your work in a press release or sound bite.

Gathering Data for Policy Research

CONSIDER THE PROBLEM confronting a researcher preparing an analysis of water pollution control programs for Blue Lake. He knows there is a dirty lake; that there is federal, state, and local legislation directed toward the end of cleaning up the lake (or preventing it from getting much dirtier); and that there is a state environmental protection office in the area that has something to do with administering some or all of the relevant antipollution policies or programs. But the researcher needs to know more. He needs to map the present policies and programs, their political environment, the way the bureaucracies function to implement them, and the criteria by which experts and laypeople evaluate them. He also needs to make some decisions about how he himself will evaluate them; then he needs to learn what data are relevant to these criteria, and finally to figure out how to obtain these data. If he is planning to recommend changes in existing programs, he must develop the evidence that will permit him to make reasonable projections of the likely outcomes. In addition, he must learn what sort of changes the present set of relevant actors might be prepared to make or are capable of making.

These are large questions, but the researcher's resources in time, energy, money, and the goodwill of potential informants and interviewers are probably not at all large. Preferably he would like to finish the study in no more than six months, let us say, and he does not want to waste the first five months simply getting his bearings. Where is he to begin? And once begun, how is he to proceed?

Part II is a revised version of an essay originally published in *Journal of Urban Analysis* 2 (1974): 117–44, by Gordon and Breach Science Publishers Ltd.

In the Beginning

The very first step is simple: Start with what you know. This injunction may seem self-evident or trivial or both. In fact, it is common for people to act in contradiction of it. Confronted by a new and challenging research task, they expect to flounder anxiously for a few weeks or months. And behold they do, for feeling stupid makes you so. Rarely is this necessary, however. A few facts, or even vague recollections, plus some intelligent reasoning can usually move the project onto firm footing surprisingly quickly. Suppose, for example, you are asked to do a policy analysis of "the future of the Wichahissic bituminous coal industry," a subject as remote from your interest or previous experience as galactic spectroscopy. You might take stock by writing a memo to yourself as follows:

1. I was probably asked to do this study because someone thinks the future of the Wichahissic bituminous coal industry is pretty bleak or else because it is looking up. If the former, the results will probably be used to justify some sort of government subsidy; if the latter, the results will be used for promotional purposes by the industry itself or by local merchants whose livelihood depends on the health of the industry.
2. The future of any industry depends in part on market demand. The demand for coal has probably been declining, partly due to the availability of substitute fuels.
3. Maybe there are high production costs that imperil the health of the industry. Could it be that coal-mining technology is underdeveloped? If so, why? Perhaps the coal fields are running out and the technology has not been developed to handle poor, as opposed to rich, deposits.
4. There were a lot of miners' strikes a few years ago. Are labor-management relations better or worse now? Are wage demands forcing the companies to go under?
5. Concerning railroads and coal, coal transportation depends on railroads. So, if the railroads are sick, could coal be well?
6. Concerning ecology and coal, coal is black and sooty and gives off a lot of smoke. Surely this is an ecological menace. Who, if anyone, is paying attention to this problem? Or is it really a problem? Coal mining destroys the beauty, and probably the ecology, of the countryside. Is this really so? Might the Sierra Club have useful data on these questions?
7. Perhaps coal is not sick, just bituminous coal. Maybe the anthracite industry is flourishing. Surely there is be a trade association of coal-mining companies with data here. Call up the nearest big coal company and find out its name and address from the public relations office.
8. Perhaps coal is okay, but Wichahissic has a problem. But then again,

Wichahissic does not seem to be as much in the news as Pokanoka, whose plight seems to be the archetype for "the depressed area." Check BLS (Bureau of Labor Statistics) for unemployment figures here.

Writing memos of this kind to yourself is useful not only at the beginning of a project but whenever you feel yourself beginning to drift toward panic or confusion. Following this initial stock taking, you should think of yourself as designing, executing, and periodically readjusting a research strategy that will exploit certain predictable changes in your potential for gaining and utilizing information:

1. *Locating relevant sources.* Over time, you decrease your uncertainty about what is worth knowing and how to learn it.
2. *Gaining and maintaining access to sources.* (a) Over time, you augment your capacity to obtain interviews from busy or hostile persons, and to obtain data that are not clearly in the public domain; (b) over time, you also—and unavoidably—use up your access to certain sources, and you must therefore conserve such an exhaustible resource for use only when the time is propitious.
3. *Accumulating background information as leverage.* Over time, you improve your capacity to interpret data and to force them out of reluctant sources, thereby increasing further your background knowledge.
4. *Protecting political credibility.* Over time, the research process itself creates an environment that will either help or hinder the adoption and implementation of your, or your client's, eventual recommendations.

The optimal strategy for managing any of these problems may conflict with the optimal strategies for dealing with the others. Each of these problems will be discussed in a separate section, the final section of this chapter being reserved for a brief treatment of dilemmas arising from trying to meet all strategic imperatives simultaneously. I assume throughout that the reader is an inexperienced policy researcher who has had academic training in the social sciences. Hence, I go to some lengths, at various points, to allude to differences between social science research methodology and the methods of policy research. I trust that the more experienced researcher will also find some profit in the arguments here, if only to conceptualize more clearly what she has already learned to do intuitively.

Another clarification about the intended audience is also in order. You start your task with certain resources and constraints, some of which are derived from your own experience and personality and others from your institutional location. Although institutional location is especially important in designing an optimal research strategy, it will not be discussed in this book. Suffice it to say that the resources and constraints of a legislative staff assistant are quite different from those of her counterpart in a bureaucratic setting and are even more dissimilar from those of one of Nader's Raiders. The strategic advice offered here is intended to be sufficiently general to meet the needs of researchers in any of these circumstances, however.

Locating Relevant Sources

Unlike most social science research, most policy research is derivative rather than original. That is, it is produced by creative play with ideas and data already developed by others. Only occasionally does the policy researcher set out to generate his or her own data or assume responsibility for inventing a bright policy idea from scratch. His or her role is preeminently discovering, collating, interpreting, criticizing, and synthesizing ideas and data that others have developed already. To be sure, social science research often works this way too, but it also places a much higher premium on originality. In a sense, the policy researcher becomes an expert on experts, "experts" here being those scholars and persons of experience who are thought to be relatively sophisticated about the policy area.

Documents and People

In policy research, almost all likely sources of information, data, and ideas fall into two general classes: documents and people. By *documents* I mean anything that has to be read: books, journal articles, newspapers and magazines, government reports, statistical archives, interoffice memoranda, position papers, bulletins, and so on. By *people* I mean both individuals and groups: The means of consulting such personal sources is typically through asking questions and listening for answers. Research on any policy problem usually entails a canvass of both types of source, though some researchers tend to overemphasize one at the expense of the other. Sometimes this tendency occurs out of habit: if the researcher starts out interviewing experts, experienced administrators, and other informed persons, he continues doing so until he comes to define "interviewing" as what his job is all about. The researcher slowly forgets the fact that the experts themselves typically obtained their expertise from documents, and that much of what administrators offer can be found in agency reports, legislative hearings, published statutes and regulations, and so on.

Another reason for getting stuck in one medium and neglecting the other is the personal preference for either passive or active modes of inquiry, that is, for libraries (or files, in an organizational setting) as opposed to fieldwork, or else a preference for less rather than more personal interaction. It is usually desirable not only to consult both types of sources (documents and people) but also to consult them in alternating order: a spate of interviewing followed by a retreat to the library followed by another round of interviewing, and so on. If for no other reason, there is probably a psychic economy in arranging and executing a fieldwork agenda in a consolidated time span, as there is in collecting and exploring a large body of documentary material.

In a more general way, however, it should be remembered that one source should be used to locate another and that this branching out can just as easily lead from one medium to the other as it can from source to source of the same type of medium. More explicitly, people lead to documents as well as to other people, and documents lead to people as well as to other documents. There are thus four basic branches on the tree of knowledge, each of which we shall discuss in turn.

People lead to people. Often one informant leads spontaneously to another by remarking during the course of an interview or conversation, "Have you seen X yet? She's very knowledgeable about . . ." This information can be stimulated by the researcher's asking questions like "Who else would be a good person to talk to about . . . ?" This might be more specific: "Who would be a good person to see in Agency Y?" For reasons of tact, one might frame the question more tentatively: "Do you think it would be advisable to talk to . . . —or do you think that would not be advisable?" Sometimes it is a good idea to ask the informant explicitly if his name can be used in seeking an appointment with the person he has suggested. This gives him an opportunity to protect himself if he does not want his name to be use and an opportunity to encourage name dropping if he believes it will serve his interests. (That is, A may wish B to know that A has spoken of him as "a knowledgeable person" or words to that effect.) Make sure that the informant provides a sufficient address or telephone number of anyone he recommends seeing so that it is possible to locate the person.

Knowing whom to stay away from is often an important by-product of inquiries like these. If the informant is trusting and wishes to be helpful, she may volunteer a cautionary aside such as, "If you do go to see X, you'll probably find him reserved if not unsympathetic." Unless X is a very important step in the developmental sequence at that moment, this might very well be a clue not to approach X until better groundwork has been laid for such a meeting. Another important by-product of such inquiries is a file of information on who is friendly, or antagonistic, to whom. Such information will be useful in constructing a map of political and administrative feasibility for any new program that the researcher might eventually propose.

People lead to documents. Just as one can ask people whom else to see or talk to, one can also ask them what else to read and how to obtain it. In visiting people in their offices, you can sometimes get useful hints by scanning the bookshelves and the papers on tables and desktops for titles and authors or agency names. Also, take all the documents away from the interview that the informant is willing to give you, even if you are not sure how relevant they are. The chances are good that you will turn up some interesting new material in the collection you eventually develop, and in any case, you may avoid a trip to the library should you later wish to quote them or to report precise bibliographical information. Finally, have yourself put on mailing lists, so as to be on the receiving end of whatever stream of reports, bulletins, newsletters, circulars, and so on are distributed by organizations operating in the policy area.

Documents lead to documents. Anyone who has ever written a substantial academic research paper in history or the social sciences has probably learned how to use one document to discover another through footnotes and bibliographies. The same procedures work in policy research. In addition, one frequently uncovers references that are incomplete from a strictly academic point of view, but that are still useful for policy research. These are references to agencies or organizations (and even individuals) that have an ongoing responsibility for or interest in the policy area. Some of these can be expected to sponsor studies, reports, position papers, and so on that will prove invaluable. You might, of course, need a certain ingenuity to find out their addresses. Fortunately, this is not a problem for most agencies, special study commissions, or task forces that operate under public auspices.

Once research is under way "documents lead to documents" in a relatively straightforward way and without much difficulty. The problem is in knowing where to start when the research effort is just beginning. Ordinarily, the researcher will want an overview of the policy area at this early point, and it is advisable to think of three rather distinct dimensions along which to take sightings: the nature of the social problem, the array of existing public and private responses to the problem, and patterns of political conflict and cooperation among the actors (both collective and individual) making those responses.

As to the first, a scholarly or semischolarly book of recent vintage is probably the best place to begin. Indeed, several such books make the best beginning. How should one find them? There are no doubt many ways, but a fairly reliable one involves thinking of an academic discipline or field that is closely related to the policy area, locating the principal scholarly journals published in that field, and then consulting the most recent issues of those journals for book reviews, footnotes, and bibliographies that report book titles of probable interest and significance.

The array of existing policy responses is best approached through identifying the leading public agency operating in the policy areas. From its periodic reports to the legislature, public relations newsletters, and special studies one can usually glean information about a wide variety of other programs and actors in the area. Sometimes these can be usefully supplemented by reports produced on the legislative side by committee staff evaluating ongoing policies or trying to justify new directions.

One cannot go through all the above scholarly and governmental publications without learning something about the pattern of political conflict and cooperation in the policy area; yet this information may still not be sufficient for the initial overview one seeks. Since politics is often a prime concern of newspaper reporters and magazine writers, consult the *New York Times* index and the principal periodical indexes for story titles that suggest coverage of such topics.

Documents lead to people. Once having read, or read about, the work done by certain experts, academic or otherwise, you might wish to consult with them face to face or by telephone. You should be wary, of course, of mistaking the nominal author of a study for the real one, particularly when she or he is a person or group in officialdom. The nominal authors of Supreme Court decisions, to take an extreme example, are the Associate Justices, but the real authors are usually their clerks, who in turn probably draw most of their arguments from the briefs filed by the attorneys on the case. Similarly, you should look behind the agency official whose name appears on the cover of a report, to locate the staff who did the work and may be named on the inside pages or referred to in a preface.

Of course, you are not interested in the names of experts alone. The nominal as opposed to the real authors of a study may be important sources of political information. Their nominal credit as authors or study participants probably reflects their political significance (in someone's eyes, at least), and their willingness to accept nominal responsibility for the work perhaps signifies their readiness to play a public relations role of some sort—and perhaps to grant interviews to peripatetic policy researchers.

Secondhand Information

To find out what Senator A is doing or thinking about a policy problem, one need not necessarily ask the senator herself. Tens or hundreds of individuals may know the answer, or at least part of the answer. Such secondhand information must be used cautiously and constantly checked for bias or error. But it is in no a priori sense inferior to information obtained firsthand, which has its own biases and factual errors. To use a legal analogy, one relies for "truth" on witnesses rather than on the defendant, who after all cannot easily or prudently be asked to testify against himself. Sometimes it makes sense to obtain firsthand information as a supplement to the other, particularly if there is reason to think that failure to do so might ultimately jeopardize the credibility of the final research product.

The use of secondhand sources is especially important in seeking political feasibility data. Suppose, for example, that you are planning to recommend that emergency ambulance services be centralized under the city police department, and you want to estimate the probable reaction of the fire chief to such a recommendation. You could ask the fire chief himself, but he might not be willing to tell the truth, especially if he were going to hold out his acquiescence in return for better terms or for some side payment. That is, he might in principle be willing to go along with the change—he might indeed be an enthusiast for it—but for bargaining purposes he might not be prepared to let on. On the other hand, he might really be against it but not be willing to let on to that either because he thinks people might call him an obstructionist. In either case, the fire chief is not an easy source of this information. Eventually it might be desirable to ask him his opinion directly, but one could probably learn as much or more by asking instead a variety of secondhand sources like a veteran city hall reporter, rank-and-file fire fighters, someone in the city manager's office, and someone from the police department.

Multiple Sources of Firsthand Information

Suppose you wish to know about the past relationship between the police and fire departments. Have they been relatively cooperative, antagonistic, or indifferent? If for some reason you do not wish to ask the fire chief, it is always possible to ask the police chief, since she has been a partner to these relations as much as the fire chief. She may have a different view or interpretation of these relationships, but she is as much a participant and her knowledge just as direct.

This principle has numerous applications. If you want to know what happened at a particular meeting to which you were denied admission (or to which you could not go for other reasons), there are many participants to query. If you want to know how one particular participant behaved at that meeting, you do not necessarily have to ask the participant. You can ask others who attended. If you wish to see a memorandum sent by Smith to Jones, you can ask either Smith or Jones, depending on which one you believe will be more agreeable—or obtain a photocopy from a third party.[1]

---

1. The notion of systematically using secondhand sources and the notion of multiple sources for firsthand information are foreign to the spirit and practice of much social science research. Social science research typically assumes that when one wants to know the mental states or the conduct of a given individual, the best source is that individual. It then worries about how to devise measuring instruments and interviews that will register these facts about the individual with the least distortion. Often this is quite appropriate for the questions about which one does basic and original research, when the object is to get pure data for pure understanding. But in policy research the problem is to get a sufficient understanding of the world to be able to make estimates about alternative courses of action. Since there is much uncertainty about the future, and so many uncontrollable variables that will enter into future action, too much precision about the past and present frequently gets in the way.

The Search for Sources and the Search for Knowledge

At the beginning of a policy research project, the researcher faces a dual uncertainty, about what she thinks she ought to know and where she can turn to learn it. These are interdependent questions, in the sense that the reduction of one type of uncertainty is both a consequence of and a condition for the reduction of the other.

Consider first what happens as the researcher clarifies her ideas about what she thinks she ought to know. Simultaneously, she is able to exclude certain sources she would otherwise have consulted, and because she knows better what her objectives are, she is able to intensify her search for sources of more certain relevance. This is the classic research model, in which ends determine means; that is, a constantly evolving set of knowledge objectives gives shape to the strategy of source selection and consultation. It is as applicable to policy research as to any other sort of social inquiry.

Its exact opposite is also applicable—and quite properly so, though many would wish to deny it. Because the cost of searching for adequate sources is so high in time and energy, when one finds a rich source it may be wise to mine it intensively, even if that decision slightly alters one's original knowledge objectives. If you wish to make recommendations to the state legislature concerning the reduction of criminal recidivism rates, for instance, the most relevant data source (recidivism in that particular state) may not be as rich—and therefore useful—as data from the bureau of criminal statistics run by some state that does an especially good job of collecting such data.

One danger in this sort of pragmatism is that you will spend too much of your time on what appears to be a rich source, not knowing that there are much richer ones just around the corner. That is why it is wise to invest a good deal of time initially in canvassing a variety of possible sources and developing a broad overview of both the policy area and what means there are to learn about it. After this initial survey, it is possible to return to sources that look unusually rich. This procedure also guards against the second, and more important, danger in letting the sources guide you: you might lose sight of more desirable and feasible knowledge objectives. In the final analysis, there must be a balance between the classic model of ends (knowledge) dictating means (sources) and the pragmatic model of ends evolving out of the means one has at hand.

Gaining Access and Engaging Assistance

In policy research, a resource of particular importance is access to informants you wish to interview. If you wish to interview Assembly Member Jones, for example, you must persuade the appointments secretary that you are on serious business and that in any event you will not be put off. You must arrange an appointment for a not-too-distant date and persist even after Jones breaks the first appointment and fails to show up for the one made in lieu of that one. If you wish to interview Jones after the first time, you must take pains to keep this possibility open, and perhaps to foster it by your conduct during the first interview.

Often it is necessary to engage the active assistance of certain informants. From the researcher's point of view, engaging such assistance is merely a special case of the problem of gaining access; it is access in a higher degree, so to speak. Such assistance is desirable especially when you are trying to collate and interpret statistical data in the possession of some agency. Often these data are in a raw state; that is, the data are in the files but need to be collated and tabulated. Sometimes the data are in a semiprocessed condition; that is, they have been collated and tabulated, but they have not been put in a format intelligible to the researcher. (They are still in a format that is intelligible to the program managers, but this format does not fully reveal the meaning of the data to the researcher.) In such a case, the researcher may wish to know about seeming inconsistencies in the classification of cases, or about the meaning of certain class designations that the managers have developed for their own decision making.

Finally, there are data that have been processed for public use but that have not been processed completely or adequately for your purposes. Suppose the intramural evaluation staff of a state penal institution, for example, has issued its annual report on releases and recidivists, but one cannot tell from the report how reliably they have ascertained the prior arrest and conviction record of the so-called first offenders. Did they rely on probation officer reports? On prison records? Records from other states? The error structure of an agency's data is often not known to the agency, and if it is, it might not be made known to the public. In this case, as in the case of raw and semiprocessed data, interpretive assistance is needed from the agency itself. How much assistance it is willing to give depends, in part at least, on how well the researcher has cultivated good working relations with the agency and its personnel.

Getting an Appointment

Why should any informant grant you, a mere policy researcher, an interview? American manners and mores provide the most compelling reasons; it is part of our definition of courtesy. If someone talks to you, even through your appointment secretary, you are supposed to talk back. Of course, the more powerful, busy, or politically defensive the personage besought, the less will be the force of simple courtesy. In such cases, you might try to appeal to a sense of noblesse oblige or, if you have a prestigious institutional affiliation, to a willingness to acknowledge your caste privileges. In addition, many people simply feel flattered by having an outsider—even a policy researcher—wanting to listen to them.

More reliable than these appeals to mere sentiment, however, is an appeal to political self-interest. Try to indicate that the outcome of your research is likely to have a bearing on the interviewee's (or her agency's) political fortunes and ambitions. It would therefore be prudent for her to be cooperative, arrange for you to hear her (or her agency's) point of view, and indeed to use the interview setting to assess the relevant political implications of your work. Of course, it may require some fast talking over the telephone, when you call for an appointment, in order to set her mind thinking in these directions. In dealing with an appointments secretary, who will probably be even less sensitive to your political cues, you might have to make your points indelicately explicit. Instead of relying on the vagaries of a telephone conversation or an appointment secretary, it might be useful to write a letter requesting an interview. In such cases, it is advisable to follow up the letter with a telephone call checking on the status of your request.

Many of the informants whom you will interview are acquainted with each other and will occasionally talk among themselves about you and your work. It is best to have such discussions serve your interests rather than work against them. You should therefore attempt to develop a reputation as a competent, knowledgeable, and energetic researcher who is likely to produce something of intellectual or political significance. The best way to develop such a reputation is actually to be such a person, but in addition, certain stratagems may prove useful. Attempt, for instance, to become a familiar face, by attending meetings and conferences that your potential informants attend, and by loitering around office cafeterias or after-hours places that they frequent. Try to impress people with your ability to gain entree to meetings that are only quasi-public in nature, and by talking in public places to important personages. Of course, all this familiarity will backfire if you appear pesky or inept, so some judiciousness is in order. Also, you should appear to be learning quickly and critically while in these settings, rather than observing passively and dully. A notebook, in which you enter notes fast and furiously, is occasionally a good stage prop as well as useful in its own right. Likewise, animated conversation, preferably observed rather than overheard, can enhance your appearance in these settings.

Do not imagine that fieldwork can proceed rapidly or smoothly. For the most part, you are the captive of other people's schedules. You can expect delays of three days to three weeks between the time you request an appointment and the appointment date—and even longer if your informant eventually breaks the appointment and reschedules it for a few weeks later. Sometimes it seems that research is mainly idle waiting! This problem is particularly acute if delay in seeing one informant is a bottleneck to seeing others. To minimize idleness, it is a good idea to have two or three independent streams of interviewing running simultaneously, so that a bottleneck in any single stream cannot halt your work altogether.

Cultivating Access

Securing repeated access to an individual or agency presents different problems from securing a one-time-only appointment. Courtesy is of almost no use here; the political motive, conversely, is critical. Since the political impact of your work on certain individuals and organizations will almost certainly be adverse, some doors will inevitably be closed to you. Beyond a certain point, there is nothing to be done about them, except to seek alternative means of entry.

A perceived political affinity helps, but by itself it is not sufficient. It is virtually impossible to secure repeated access to people unless they trust and like you. To put it another way, securing repeated access depends in large part on building rapport with the objects of your study. Building rapport takes time, especially if you are not inclined to appear more friendly and congenial than you really feel. Rapport follows most of all from simple exposure. You should think of yourself as an anthropologist who has to spend several months living among the tribe she is studying before being allowed to observe certain sacred rituals and practices. Thus you may find it useful to make repeated visits to the agency, say, either for interviewing or for some other purpose, like document gathering and reading, and to use such opportunities to give yourself as much exposure as possible.

Rapport is especially important for engaging assistance of the sort described above. Almost invariably, whoever actually assists you in collating and interpreting agency data will see himself as "doing you a favor," regardless of how insistent his superiors have been that he make his services freely and generously available to you. As part of the conditions for such a "favor," you must reciprocate with expressions of gratitude and sympathy for his "going out of his way."

Another case in which the objects of one's research provide active assistance is in feeding unsolicited tips and leads or other types of information. This does not happen often, but when it does it can be very helpful. A cooperative informant might mail you a copy of a speech she has recently given, knowing that it will be of interest to you. Or she might see to it that you are put on the list of invitees to a banquet at which you will be able to meet a number of potential informants in an informal setting. To a certain extent, this sort of assistance can be encouraged simply by letting people know that it will be welcomed. It can be facilitated by having a telephone and fax number, and e-mail and postal addresses, where you can be reached or where messages can be left. It may even be useful to have business cards printed with this information. Relative to other research expenses this one is quite small and can return high dividends.

Exhausting Access

Access can be exhausted, too, not just cultivated and built up. Whereas in some cases repeated exposure helps the researcher build rapport, in others exposure simply tears it down. In the extreme instance of the latter, one exposure is all the relationship will bear; this commonly occurs when the informant is defensive or antagonistic, or when he is extremely busy and cannot easily be imposed upon. Other instances are intermediate: the informant is willing to grant two but not three interviews—or three but not four. When access to an informant can be exhausted relatively quickly, it is generally wise to defer interviewing her until relatively late in the research; principally because your accumulated knowledge will put you in a better position to interview such an informant.

Usually, deferring interviews with such informants inflicts no hardship on the researcher, since in the earliest stages of the interviewing, research can be conducted by talking with the legion of lower-level officials and administrative assistants, public relations officer, and so on. A very rich information source is to be found in retired officials and in agency officials who are part of a dissident faction.[2] These are rich sources at any time but are especially valuable in the earlier stages of research when it is thought advantageous to defer approaches to more highly placed figures in the political establishment.

The researcher's reputation is also susceptible to being exhausted. It is perhaps not in danger of being lost, strictly speaking, so much as it is vulnerable to being transformed into an unwanted and detrimental reputation. Instead of being thought of as fair-minded, discreet, intelligent, and self-possessed, one can get the reputation of being partisan, a tale bearer, a dope, or a dupe. The best way to avoid such an undesirable reputation is to eschew partisanship and indiscretion and, as we have already indicated, to actually be intelligent and self-possessed.

Acquiring and Using Leverage

Policy research, in its completed form, becomes a political resource. Whatever its merits or demerits as a piece of rational analysis, it becomes more than that. It becomes a justification for certain parties to attack others or defend themselves against attack, hence a weapon of persuasion in a war of propaganda. Although the tone and format of published policy research are typically neutral and disinterested, everyone recognizes that the research may be and often is used for political purposes, either by the author or by others. Hence informants are highly sensitive to the political implications of whatever they tell you. How an informant treats you depends in large part on how she thinks your work will be brought to bear on her personal or political interests.

---

2. My former Goldman School colleague William Niskanen relates that colonels twice passed over for promotion to general were a favored source for civilian policy analysts like himself in the U.S. Defense Department.

Being wary of the possible political implications of what they might reveal, informants may be reluctant to talk freely and honestly. The researcher initially does well to assume that all interviewees confront this problem, even though it may not be known to what degree. In the more extreme cases, it may be necessary to use leverage against the interviewee of various and subtle kinds. Before we turn to the problem in its most severe manifestations, though, I will set forth a basic strategy for conducting policy research interviews in general.

Energy Plus Direction Equals Information

The interview is a process of interaction carried on between the informant and the researcher. The principal source of energy for this process should be the informant, not the researcher. The latter should stimulate the former to talk and to keep on talking, and once a suitable momentum has been attained, the researcher's role should be to steer, to redirect, to slow down, and to cross-examine. This procedure should give the informant a feeling that she has some power to define the situation and control the interview process—which she certainly does—a feeling that makes her more comfortable in speaking her mind.

Although the exact means to stimulate the informant are quite various, the presumed political significance of the research provides some clues to how generally to proceed. You may be able to assist the informant to see in the research a vehicle of favorable public relations for himself or for some institution or cause with which he is associated. It is safe to say that most politicians, administrators, and important staff feel that much of their best and most valuable work is done behind the scenes and therefore does not come to the attention of those constituencies that would otherwise express appropriate appreciation. They are often correct about this, and about the corollary assumption that the researcher and the research product may make their good works visible and earn the appreciation to which they are entitled.

A related but distinguishable motive for an informant to talk expansively is to "tell his side of the story." Whereas the public relations motive connotes a positive, or affirmative, attitude, telling one's side of the story is more defensive. The informant's implicit assumption here is that relevant constituencies are critical of his agency's conduct or policy, and that false or misleading or insufficient information is in some degree responsible for this situation. He might hope to correct the situation by expostulating aggressively, trying to put information in its "proper" perspective, or by clarifying and interpreting information that is already public. Hence, he might welcome the researcher as someone who will be a vehicle for his opinions and information. At the very least, he might see the researcher as someone who will "put on the record" what he has to say, even if the researcher should prove to be unsympathetic. Ordinarily, the informant's goals in this respect are not incompatible with those of the researcher, and there will be no reasons why the researcher could not energize the informant's discussion by holding forth this promise of getting him on the record. Of course, the researcher must take pains to indicate, usually in subtle ways, that she is fair-minded and also sufficiently knowledgeable and intelligent to be able to put the informant on the record responsibly and adequately.

In most social science research involving interviews, it is assumed that the interviewer is, as much as possible, a neutral instrument recording data emitted by the respondent. In general, this is an inappropriate model for policy research interviews. The informant assumes that the researcher is anything but a neutral instrument, since the whole object of the researcher's work is to arrive at some policy recommendations, and it is foolish for the researcher to try to appear in such an ill-fitting disguise. Thus the researcher need not fear to probe the informant with provocative and even argumentative questions or comments. These cause an informant to sharpen her wits and tone up her memory and may raise her psychic metabolism sufficiently to infuse energy into the whole interview process. If done with proper finesse, the informant will appreciate the stimulation. The researcher's finesse, of course, consists of being argumentative without sounding, or being, closed-minded or hostile. It is a good idea to broach argumentative remarks in such a way that the informant can retreat gracefully from the topic at hand into another topic, should she wish to do so, thus keeping her energy level up rather than dropping into an embarrassed taciturnity.

Most interviews are conducted at the informant's place of work. Sometimes, however, a more informal setting should be arranged, such as a restaurant or cafe. The method of note taking should be compatible with such an informal setting, perhaps on the back of an envelope handily stored in one's pocket for just such occasions.

Apart from energizing the informant, the interviewer's other main function in the interview process is to steer the informant onto topics of interest to the researcher himself (although unexpectedly interesting material often does turn up when the informant is allowed to take the lead completely for a while). How can this be done? First, it is necessary to interfere in the informant's conversation stream simply to reestablish the researcher's right to speak and also to temporarily slow the informant down without making her lose too much momentum. This can be done by interrupting with a short string of easily answered factual questions pertaining to the subject matter previously under discussion. The content of these questions, or at least the last one in the string, should be such as to work a transition to the next topic the researcher has in mind.

Suppose, for example, that you are interviewing the integrated-social-services coordinator in your county and he is telling you about his agency's relations with the county's chief administrative officer (CAO). You have heard enough on this subject and you now want to steer him onto his agency's current budget request to HUD. The conversation might go like this:

> *Informant:* . . . so you see we've had a devil of a fight with the CAO all the way. Maybe it's not her fault, of course, the Board of Supervisors being so conservative and the CAO needing support for her reappointment . . .
>
> *Researcher:* [Interrupting] Yes, she is up for reappointment this year, isn't she?
>
> *Informant:* Yes.
>
> *Researcher:* Well at least she doesn't control your budget, does she?
>
> *Informant:* True enough.
>
> *Researcher:* But HUD does—and how are your relations with them? Do you get pretty much what you ask for from them, in the way of a budget, I mean?

The point is not to disguise from the informant the fact that you are trying to steer him away from one topic and onto another, although sometimes this is desirable and should be attempted. The point is really to help him move from one topic to another without having to lose momentum or to feel awkward. Indeed, he will sometimes feel trapped on a topic that he himself would prefer to leave, and your job at such moments is to help him maneuver off the subject. If you cannot think of where you wish to lead him next, just think of a subject that is, at least, not implausible and that is not too demanding emotionally or intellectually. While you go in slow motion through that topic, both you and the informant will have a chance to collect your thoughts and feelings preparatory to moving to the next matter of serious concern.

Involving the informant in discussions of personalities is typically a matter of some delicacy. Above all, the informant must be reassured that you are not turning the interview into a gossip session, that he is not a purveyor of gossip, and that you are not a seeker of it. This can be done by first introducing the name of the personality in a neutral, usually factual, context:

> *Researcher:* A few moments ago you mentioned the Southside Community Health League. Dr. Green has been head of that for about a year now—or is it two?
>
> *Informant:* Probably closer to two.
>
> *Researcher:* Maybe it just seems shorter because I remember Dr. Black, her predecessor, so vividly.
>
> *Informant:* Yes, Black was quite a leader there.

>   *Researcher:* Seems people have been more critical of Green—though I
> have heard quite complimentary things from some sources.
>   *Informant:* Yes, she's pretty controversial. She's certainly a competent
> administrator and been pretty nice to us—though we deal mainly with
> her deputy, Mr. White.
>   *Researcher:* How come?

Thus the conversation is turned to personalities by a sequence of small steps, in which each participant encourages the other and in which both assume responsibility for whatever gossipy quality may eventually threaten to intrude. Since personalities are such a sensitive topic, it is even a good idea for the researcher to sprinkle his conversation with allusions to people about whom he may have no desire to question the informant. When the researcher does desire to pursue a discussion of a particular personality, this procedure makes the discussion seem less of a departure from the normal course of topics.

Of course, if the informant has unpleasant things to say about the personality under discussion, the researcher might take pains to indicate his own social, personal, and political distance from the individual. In the above excerpt, for example, the researcher has referred to "Dr. Green" and has indicated his distance by suggesting his unfamiliarity with certain particulars of Green's career. A contrary course might be followed if the informant has flattering things to say about the individual in question, though it is always a little risky to appear very close to anybody lest it arouse suspicions of partiality about the researcher.

The Defensive Informant

Occasionally one encounters an informant who is irrevocably committed to a defensive posture, for whom "No comment" is the primary defense, and calculated evasion is the fallback position. Try to diagnose this problem very early in the interview and to reassess your goals for the interview in light of this situation. You should concentrate on gaining information about specific questions that this informant is able to answer but that are probably not answerable by any other source. Since so much of your energies will have to go into the cracking of the informant's defenses, you should concentrate them on very specific objectives. Once these are in mind, you should begin to probe for them right away.

Once all these preliminary assessments are out of the way, and the interview has turned to specifics, the use of leverage is in order. First, let the informant understand as quickly as possible that you are aware of his defensive posture, and signal that you do not intend to be put off by it. You might try to communicate that his defensiveness will not help him, that you know too much already to be shunted aside, and that you have access to other sources who have already told you much and to still others who are willing to tell you more. Indicate that these may be more prejudicial to his interests than his own revelations would be, and that he therefore has nothing to lose, and perhaps something to gain, by honest answers. A certain amount of bluffing is sometimes possible and necessary, though to be sure there are obvious risks in this tactic. It is always better to actually know as much as you pretend to know, and to have access to the sources you claim to have access to, than merely to bluff. Here is a sample of such an interview, with the head of a prominent local insurance company whom the researcher is pressing hard:

Researcher: One thing I'd like to get more information about is the problem insurance companies have writing policies for merchants in so-called ghetto areas.

Informant: [Silence. Pause.]

Researcher: I mean, there may be problems because these policies are risky business propositions.

Informant: [Silence. Pause.]

Researcher: People say they are risky, anyway. Do underwriters in this area consider them risky?

Informant: I can't really say for sure.

Researcher: Well, some people in the Black Merchants Association claim that insurance companies won't write policies for them at all, that they've been classed as "unacceptable risks."

Informant: I don't really know—insurance writing is the science of risks, isn't it?

Researcher: [Decides that informant will provide no information on insurance industry doctrines or practices in general, or on the local under-writers in particular. Guesses that informant will be unwilling to discuss the doctrines, or rules, applied by his own company, and that she should therefore concentrate solely on gathering information about the practices of informant's company.] Perhaps I can clarify my question by being more concrete. In your own Bedrock Casualty Company, are applicants ever turned down because they are thought to be unacceptable risks?

Informant: I can't say for sure. I'm not that close to the operating de-tails of our very large company.

Researcher: Of course. [To signal she will not be put off] You, or per-haps your secretary, could arrange for me to talk to someone at that level, though, couldn't you? [Seeking a different leverage point] But tell me about the category of "unacceptable risks." Does Bedrock Casualty tell its salespeople that the company will insure any premises provided the insured pays a high enough premium? [Shifting the terms of the question to throw informant off guard] Or is there a limit on how high a premium the company will set?

Informant: Well, we do not like to charge exorbitant premiums, of course . . .

Researcher: [Interrupting] So within the existing limits on premiums there might in fact be businesses too risky to insure—hence "unacceptable"? [Holding to offensive] How about cancellations? Has Bedrock canceled or refused to renew any policies of ghetto merchants even though they have not filed any claims recently? This is another thing the Black Merchants Association has been complaining about.

Informant: [Deciding researcher knows more than he had thought and deciding to get preemptive protection against the Black Merchants Association's allegations] Well, yes, we have canceled a few, in the more riot-prone areas, and refused to renew other policies in that area. We had no choice; we stood to lose a lot of money in case of any trouble.

Researcher: [Graciously ignoring this "confession," and trying to induce informant to tell his side of the story] Of course, that's quite understandable. I think most people recognize this problem. [Now taking aim on a single statistic, the proportion of all Bedrock policies in ghetto neighborhoods canceled or not renewed in the last two years] In the past, have you written many policies in that area?

Informant: Yes, we've done quite a bit, in the past anyway.

Researcher: You still do insure some business over there, don't you?

Informant: Yes, we do, though as I say, I'm not too close to the operating details . . .

Researcher: [Interrupting] Could you estimate what proportion of your policy holders from, say, two years ago you continue to insure? Is it 80 percent, 20 percent? Just to give me some rough idea.

Informant: Well, it would certainly be a lot closer to 80 than 20 but I really don't know.

Researcher: [Deciding that this would be an interesting datum and that it is worth pursuing vigorously] Can we find out?

Informant: Not easily. It's not in any files anywhere in that form, and it would be awfully difficult to find out.

Researcher: [Not believing that it would be very difficult, and deciding that she is willing to contribute her own labor to searching the files, if necessary, resorts to a bluff] People have the impression that Bedrock is less inclined to write policies for ghetto merchants than other companies in this area. I don't know where the facts come from—but I think some lawyers connected with the Black Merchants Association have been looking into legal aspects . . .

Informant: What? I'm sure we are no worse, or different, than any other company in town! I'd like to see these so-called facts!

Researcher: If I get any further clarification on that, I'd be happy to let you know. Meanwhile, I'd be willing to help out in whatever way you like in getting this information together concerning your own company's record in this field.

We interrupt this scene without a conclusion because, however it turns out, the researcher has done the best she could. The president of Bedrock Casualty may deliver the sought-for information, or he may not. Good interviewing strategy and tactics do not guarantee success, especially when the odds are weighted against the researcher to begin with.[3]

One common ploy used by a defensive informant is to reel out masses of irrelevant statistics and facts. These can easily swamp a naively data-worshipping researcher. Another ploy is to ramble garrulously about side issues, meanwhile running out the clock on whatever time limit he has set for the interview. The researcher's best defense against these ploys is to be able to recognize them for what they are.

If your own leverage fails, and if certain information is sufficiently important to you, you may be able to use someone else's. A graduate student researcher based in the university may have little leverage with determinedly defensive bureaucrats, for instance, but a legislator, or her staff assistant, will almost certainly have more. Hence, as a last resort, the student might persuade a sympathetic legislator to help out. Sometimes a newspaper reporter might be of assistance. Perhaps an established group can help. The local medical society, for example, might be able to get information from the county hospital administrator about hospital policies that no academic researcher, and possibly not even a county supervisor, could get.

A significant constraint on using leverage is the desirability of maintaining

---

3. The researcher's bluffing tactic in this scene is of debatable morality. Although I believe it would be unethical in most circumstances, there are occasions when it would be justified. This is one of them. In this case, the Bedrock president seeks to withhold proprietary information. Does he have a right to do so? Normally, yes. But this right has to be weighed against the injustice of depriving ghetto merchants of a nearly essential prerequisite for doing business when they might be perfectly willing to meet reasonable price terms for acquiring the insurance (perhaps with government or philanthropic assistance). The researcher here has an arguable right to try to combat this injustice. Given that right, does she also have the right to use deception? The use of explicit deception on the part of the researcher is balanced by the use of implicit (covert) deception on the part of the president.

cordial relations with whatever agency or individual is being pried apart. The researcher runs a clear risk of alienating the objects of his leverage tactics. With respect to a given study, this problem can be mitigated by postponing the more offensive tactics until relatively late, when the study is less vulnerable to being undermined by the offended party. The problem is more difficult, however, when the researcher envisions a long-term relationship with the agency or individual under scrutiny, one lasting well beyond the conclusion of the present research effort. In such cases, no doubt, certain information will have to be sacrificed to preserving a modicum of goodwill for the future.

Protecting Credibility

Like social science research, policy research is eventually subject to criticism on intellectual grounds. But unlike social science research, it is much more vulnerable on political grounds and, indeed, is vulnerable to attack by the very subjects of the study. In social science research the subjects rarely become significant critics of the product, but in policy research their criticism is inevitable. Therefore, the researcher should take steps to protect the ultimate political credibility of his work from politically motivated as well as strictly intellectual attack.

Policy Research Aims at Approximate Truths

In contrast to social science research, the primary goal of policy research is not intellectual enlightenment (either of the researcher or of her professional colleagues), though enlightenment is inevitably a by-product. The goal is to improve one's understanding of the policy problem, and of possible means of coping with it, to the point where it is possible to advocate a responsible course of action. Thus, policy research takes aim at broad and complex phenomena and is typically satisfied by very gross approximations of "truth," in contrast to social science research, which typically seeks more refined interpretations of narrowly circumscribed problems. The gross and approximate character of policy research is an open invitation to politically inspired criticism. How can the researcher protect herself?

For one thing, she should attempt to touch base with anyone (or any institutional interest) who might later try to undermine the report by claiming to have been ignored. Indeed, it is a good idea to preempt such claims by quoting the party in the report, as evidence of a sort that the party's views were taken into account. For instance, if the researcher is going to recommend alterations in the way superintendents are selected in a given school district, it would be best to interview representatives from the local association of school administrators and from the local chapters of the National Education Association and the American Federation of Teachers. Spokespersons for these groups may have interesting opinions to contribute to the research project, but even if they do not, by consulting them the researcher gains protection against their criticisms should they decide to oppose the recommendations in her report. It may even be useful to send out a preliminary copy to these interests for reviews.

Second, one should seek out "experts" or others with political or intellectual authority to whom to attribute views, opinions, estimates, and so on, about which the researcher feels especially uncertain. Quoting published sources is one way of making such attributions, and quotations from interviews are another. In addition, the researcher should plan to have experts lined up who will be willing to speak up in support of her work once it becomes public. If people are quoted in the report as having a view on this or that, they become natural targets for inquiring journalists or political decision makers, to whom they also have an incentive to defend their quoted views.

Third, the researcher should pay special attention to potential opponents and identify which propositions they are likely to attack. These should be bolstered by expert quotations in advance and a polite reference made to the existence of counterarguments without at the same time giving them too much space or prominence. The very opponents who can be projected to raise these objections subsequently should be quoted, in order to defuse their claims that their arguments or positions were ignored. (There may be additional psychological advantages to the balanced or two-sided presentation, sheerly in terms of propaganda and persuasion directed at the reader.)

Statistical data are often useful for buttressing credibility. Used for this purpose, statistics play a documentation rather than an information role. They are used to document the validity of generalizations that political opponents might otherwise criticize, even though their truth is abundantly evident through more impressionistic sources. It is one thing to assert, for instance, that "we are experiencing a galloping inflation" and another to assert that "inflation is occurring at an annual rate of 5.5 percent."

The Risks of Premature Exposure

Politicians and policy researchers work on different timetables. Not infrequently the former call for "results" well before the research is in any sense finished. Even if no one demands results, moreover, unexpected opportunities often do present themselves before the researcher's work is close enough to being finished so that he could seize the auspicious moment to present the results.

One possible strategy is to map out (as much as possible) the timetable of potential political demands and to arrange your research timetable in at least partial correspondence. An additional strategy is to prepare yourself as quickly as possible with answers to the crudest kinds of questions that might be asked of you. Since these are generally the kinds of answers politicians need and want anyway, you might as well have them early in the course of your research. Finally, it is important to line up your supporting experts early, as well as to touch base with potential opponents. Since, once again, these contacts must be made eventually, there is good reason to make them early rather than late.

Strategic Dilemmas of Policy Research

By way of summary and conclusion, let us consider the question: Which informants should be approached when? Answering this question forces a useful return to most of the issues covered earlier.

We may divide the "when" part of the question into "relatively early" and "relatively late" in the course of the research project. Approach relatively early:

1. Persons who are likely to facilitate your search for rich information sources;
2. Powerful persons who directly or by your reputed connection with them will facilitate your access to sources;
3. Knowledgeable persons, who will provide you with the information you need to hedge against premature political exposure of your work, and whose information will contribute to your capacity to exert leverage against defensive interviewees;
4. Friendly experts, who will contribute to your political credibility in case of premature political exposure;
5. Potential opponents, with whom you touch base in order to hedge against premature political exposure.

Approach relatively late:

1. Hostile or defensive informants against whose tactics a prior buildup of leverage is desirable;
2. Busy informants, to whom you might lose access permanently once you have seen them and about whom you are not sufficiently informed to interview early;
3. Potential opponents, especially if powerful, who might try to ruin access to others and thereby cripple your research efforts;
4. Administrators who have knowledge of potential trouble spots but who

will be unwilling to point them out until it appears to be in their self-interest.

There is one obvious contradiction between these two lists (approach potential opponents early and late) and several others that are not quite so obvious. Often it is the busy and the defensive informants who are also in the best position to facilitate the search for sources, open doors, and provide useful information. Top agency administrators, for instance, have plentiful experience with the policy problem under investigation and can provide easy access to sources, but they also have a vested interest in maintaining the status quo or something very close to it. In any event, they may not take kindly to having their activities scrutinized too carefully by an outsider. Other similar examples can easily be called to mind. There is in principle no way to reconcile these incompatible prescriptions of whom to approach early and whom late. The researcher will have to consider the full details of her particular situation and then balance the risks and rewards inherent in any given choice. There is no way of avoiding such trade-offs, and the skilled policy researcher should simply make them consciously rather than inadvertently.

"Smart (Best) Practices" Research: Understanding and Making Use of What Look like Good Ideas from Somewhere Else

IT IS ONLY SENSIBLE to see what kinds of solutions have been tried in other jurisdictions, agencies, or locales. One looks for those that appear to have worked pretty well, tries to understand exactly how and why they might have worked, and evaluates their applicability to one's own situation. In many circles this process is known as *best practices research*. Simple and commonsensical as this process sounds, it presents many methodological and practical pitfalls. Part III helps you avoid the pitfalls and offers tips on how get the most payoff from your search for best practices.

Have Realistic Expectations

First, don't be misled by the *best* in best practices research. Rarely will you have any confidence that some helpful-looking practice is actually the best among all those that are addressed to the same problem or opportunity. The extensive and careful research needed to document a claim of best will almost never have been done. Usually, you will be looking for what, more modestly, might be called good practices.

But even this claim might be too grand. Often you can't even be sure that what appears to be a good practice is actually good in the sense that it is solving or ameliorating the problem to which it is nominally addressed. Appearances can be very deceiving. On closer inspection, it often turns out that a supposedly good practice is not solving the problem at all. Inadequate measurement plus someone's rose-colored glasses was simply producing the illusion of mitigating the problem.

It may also turn out that, even if good effects have truly occurred, the allegedly good practice had little or nothing to do with producing them. Finally, innocently extrapolating from a setting where a good practice has indeed worked well to settings that differ in little-understood but important ways could lead to weak, perverse, or otherwise damaging results.

None of these problems is decisive, though. If it does nothing else, a foray into "best practices research" usually turns up interesting ideas, including ideas about what does *not* work as well as what does. The challenge for the researcher is to figure out what an idea is and what makes it interesting.

"Smart Practices"

An interesting idea embedded in some practice is what I would term a *smart practice.* I prefer the term *smart practice* to *best practice* or even *good practice* because it underlines the fact that any practice worth such special attention ought usually to have something clever about it. It is this something clever that the researcher must analyze, characterize in words, and appraise for its applicability to the local situation.

Free Lunches

One way of being clever is getting something for nothing. Contrary to the dictum that there is no such thing as a free lunch, creative policymakers and policy implementers invest quite a lot of energy in looking for just such comestibles. Often, they are successful. To understand how this can be, consider the free lunch cornucopia produced by the natural sciences and engineering. The energy stored in the chemical bonds in a cup of gasoline can run a car for a few miles provided one knows how to access that energy and channel it. Pulleys and levers supply "mechanical advantage." Bacteria happily eat and destroy the organic crud in a city's wastewater almost for free. All these materials, devices, and conditions represent getting a lot of "something" for nothing or for relatively little. The source of all these boons is simply Mother Nature.

In the social world, the sources of something for nothing are usually less tangible and less directly gifts of Mother Nature, but they are no less real. The invisible hand of the market creates social value where only individual pursuit of self-interest had once been and, metaphorically at least, operates without charge. Alphabetical ordering permits people to find information in a fraction of the time it would have taken had there been no such ordering. Queuing at bus stops is easy to understand, is usually fair, and makes life better for everybody.

In the world of policy and management there are no doubt fewer and less delectable free lunches than in the marketplace or in some information storage facility or at a bus stop, but they are there. All the examples of "opportunities" described in Box I.I (Part I, p. 6) and reproduced here in Box III.I (p. 74) for the reader's convenience, have this quality. They have the *latent potential* to generate something of public value relatively cheaply.[1] One might say that the difference between the (high) value created and the (low) cost, and risk, of producing it represents a free lunch.[2]

Opportunities don't deliver up their latent value without some additional work, however. This work is done by the "practices" that take advantage of their potentialities, and these typically cost something and are subject to various vulnerabilities as well. However, the smarter they are, the more value they can manage to extract at lower cost and risk. Here are some examples of candidates for smart practice status—candidates, that is, because to my knowledge they have not all been subjected to the extensive empirical testing needed to confirm such status:

- *A "high-expectations" welfare-to-work program* in the early 1990s before the 1996 federal welfare reform act. A prototype is the Greater Avenues to Independence (GAIN) program I studied in Riverside County, California. Unlike most other welfare-to-work programs, the Riverside program set high expectations about work for GAIN participants in two senses. In many different ways, it signaled participants that program staff had confidence in (high expectations of) their ultimate success in getting a job and getting off welfare. This confidence was intended as an antidote to the low self-esteem, and consequent low effort to reattach themselves to the labor force, of many participants. Staff also signaled—and expressed in program rules about early and diligent job search, as well as through a variety of formal and informal pressures—that "society expected" welfare participants to shape up and take responsibility for their own financial well-being. The Riverside GAIN program designed its recruitment, training, performance appraisal, and other administrative systems to support this high-expectations philosophy.[3] In effect the high-expectations model took advantage of the natural energies to solve their own problems that program managers assumed to be latent in the program participants.

---

1. On the nature of "public value," see Mark H. Moore, *Creating Public Value: Strategic Management in Government* (Cambridge, Mass.: Harvard University Press, 1996).
2. Risks come in several varieties. See the section "Generic Vulnerabilities."
3. "Implementing a Paternalist Welfare-to-Work Program," in Lawrence Mead, ed., *The New Paternalism: Supervisory Approaches to Poverty* (Washington, D.C.: Brookings Institution, 1997), 248–78.

BOX III.I.   SOME GENERIC OPPORTUNITIES FOR SOCIAL IMPROVEMENT THAT OFTEN GO UNNOTICED

By-products of personal aspirations. It is possible to structure new incentives or create new opportunities for personal advantage or satisfaction that can indirectly result in social benefit (e.g., offering to share the benefits of cost-reducing innovations with public sector employees who conceive them and implement them).

Complementarity. Two or more activities can be joined so that each makes the other more productive (e.g., public works construction and combating unemployment).

Development. A sequence of activities or operations may have the potential to be arranged so as to take advantage of a developmental process (e.g., assessing welfare clients for employability and vocational interest before, rather than after, sending them out on a job search).

Exchange. There are unrealized possibilities for exchange that would increase social value. We typically design policies to exploit those that simulate marketlike arrangements (e.g., pollution permit auctions, and arrangements to reimburse an agency for services it renders another agency's clients or customers).

Multiple functions. A system can be designed so that one feature can be used to perform two or more functions (e.g., when a tax administrator dramatizes an enforcement case in such a way as both to deter potential violators and to reassure nonviolators that they are not being made into suckers for their honesty).

Nontraditional participants. Line-level employees of public agencies often have knowledge of potential program improvements that could usefully be incorporated into the agencies' policies and operations. The same is true of the agencies' customers or clients or the parties that they regulate.

Rationalization. Purely technical rationalization of a system is possible (e.g., shortening queues by deliberate spacing of arrival times, or creating contracts to solidify informal agreements that are vulnerable to decay and misunderstanding).

Rummaging. By rummaging mentally, one might discover novel uses in seemingly improbable but readily available materials (e.g., using the automobile registration system as a vehicle for carrying out voter registration as well).

Underutilized capacity. An example, in many communities, is school facilities that are utilized for relatively limited purposes for only part of the day and for only part of the year—although school officials would be quick to warn that using this capacity without harming school functions is not always easy.

- *Reading One-to-One.* This is a tutoring program for children in Grades 1–3 who have fallen badly behind in learning to read English. It was created by George Farkas, of the Social Sciences faculty of the University of Texas at Arlington, and involves systematic instruction in phonemic awareness, one-to-one tutoring by a well-trained tutor, and highly structured feedback and supervision. It was first tried out in Dallas and then spread to Houston and a number of other cities. Like all phonemics-based programs, it recognizes that English orthography does not map sounds in a systematic or logical way and that it is at some point necessary for learners to master the decoding and encoding rules actually in use. It takes advantage of the fact that children's early failures in reading that come from neglect of phonemic awareness are reversible by regular tutoring. It also takes advantage of the emotional bonding that comes with the one-to-one tutoring relationship. The simplicity and systematization of the teaching materials, teaching methods, and administrative oversight system make the program easily replicable and keep the costs relatively low.[4]
- *Sharing maintenance responsibilities for a neighborhood park* between the local parks department and the residents of the neighborhood. Nonprofit organizations often spring up to provide services beyond those provided by the public sector when there is demand for services of a nonstandard sort not provided by the public agency (e.g., same-sex schools, abortion clinics). An extension of the basic idea is a partnership in which the public sector supplies certain resources that are not only supplementary but also complementary. In many a city, the city government provides the parkland and the neighbors provide some or all of the labor to make the land more serviceable in some way. This practice takes advantage of two interesting potentialities. One is the potential for gains from trade between two parties. The second is the use of what is, in effect, barter, in a situation where there are administrative and political barriers to organizing the transaction in cash.
- *The "expenditure control budget,"* adopted first in the city of Fairfield, California, and publicized by David Osborne and Ted Gaebler in *Reinventing Government.*[5] As originally conceived and implemented, this budget gave each department the same basic mission and the same budget as the previous year (with an inflation adjustment) but abolished the line-

---

4. George Farkas, "Reading One-to-One: An Intensive Program Serving a Great Many Students While Still Achieving Large Effects." In Jonathan Crane, ed., *Social Programs That Work* (New York: Russell Sage Foundation Press, 1998), 75–109.
5. David Osborne and Ted Gaebler, *Reinventing Government: How the Entrepreneurial Spirit Is Transforming the Public Sector* (Reading, Mass.: Addison-Wesley, 1992).

item specification of objects of expenditure and permitted the department to keep any savings and reinvest them in other mission-related activities. This approach took advantage of the superior technical and opera-
tional knowledge of program implementers relative to that of elected
officials and bureaucrats in fiscal control agencies.

- *Milestone payments to nonprofit service contractors.* In 1992 the Oklahoma
  Department of Rehabilitation Services began paying nonprofit contractors for the rehabilitation milestones that mental health clients could
  achieve en route to higher levels of employability.[6] The clients got to par-
  ticipate in assessing whether the milestones had been met. The milestone
  system also permitted contractors to claim reimbursement from the state
  on a more accelerated schedule than they had previously been able to do.
  By taking advantage of the motivating power of self-interest, the milestone payment system motivated better performance from the nonprofits.
  It also provided greater transparency than more traditional fee-for-service
  arrangements, under which the funding agency did not know much
  about the quality of the service provided.

- Hennepin County, Minnesota, arranged for mental retardation clients of
  the county vocational rehabilitation program to sort and recycle discarded
  auto batteries of concern to the county's environmental management
  agency.[7] Thus, the programs took advantage of production complementar-
  ities between physical and human "assets" that they could deploy.

I have made a point, in describing each of these supposedly smart practices,
of saying that the practice "takes advantage" of something. This is a linguistic
device for ensuring that in analyzing how the practice "works," we make sure to
focus on those aspects of its "works" that are central, that is, on the fact that the
practice aims to exploit, to take advantage of, some latent opportunity for creating
value on the cheap.

Breaking Loose from Conventions and Assumptions

Another way of being clever is not so much technical—finding those free
lunches—as ideological and psychological. It involves disrespecting conventional

---

6. This program was a 1997 finalist in the Ford Foundation/Kennedy School of Government
   (KSG) Innovations in American Government competition. My source for information
   about it was the Innovations program files.
7. This was a Ford/KSG semifinalist. Sandford Borins, *Innovating with Integrity: How Local
   Heroes Are Transforming American Government* (Washington, D.C.: Georgetown University
   Press, 1998), 200; also, personal communication with Hennepin County program managers.

boundaries. In the world of public policy and management, this sometimes involves challenging assumptions anchored in value commitments. More often, it involves assumptions about what value commitments—such as "democracy" or "accountability" or "justice"—are actually required to implement them effectively. In the high-expectations welfare-to-work model, for instance, Riverside's was one of relatively few programs prior to the mid-1990s that decided it was proper to articulate the value premises that underlay its approach to case management. To take another example, since the late 1980s we have begun to shake loose the assumption that just because some good or service ought to be *financed* through taxation it ought also to be *produced or delivered* by governmental employees. Hence, we can contemplate contracting out to the nonprofit or even the profit-seeking sectors for such traditionally "governmental" functions as primary education, correctional institution construction and management, and welfare-to-work programming.[8]

Characterizing and Observing the "Practice"

What does it mean to characterize a "practice" well or poorly? For free-lunch-type smart practices, we can say the practice is "whatever takes advantage of—or exploits—the latent opportunity to create value on the cheap."[9] But let us try to say more about how to characterize this "whatever."

Characterizing the Elements of a Practice

Distinguish between elements that are "essential" and those that are "supportive." The essential elements are also the ones that do the basic causal work of the practice, that is, produce the valued results of the practice. These elements are essential in both a definitional and a causal sense. Consider the milestones payment program in Oklahoma. Although observers could reasonably differ, I would say that the essential elements are a reasonable method for defining milestones, an officially sanctioned contract describing milestones, documents attesting that milestones have been met, and a method for verifying the achievements claimed in the documents. Perhaps it was also helpful, in the Oklahoma experience as it would be elsewhere, to educate the state office responsible for overseeing contracts in the philosophy of the new system. But this and other

---

8. Whether or not contracting out is a smart practice, it is highly controversial, I might add.
9. With minor adjustments the same analysis can also be applied to "practices" whose "smartness" derives from their departure from convention.

such supporting elements—such as educating elected officials about the value of the new approach—we should not think of as definitionally or causally essential to "the practice." We should think of them as *supportive*—worth talking about in any account of how the practice can be made to work relatively better and/ or can be prevented from failing. In many circumstances, these are likely to be the institutions, personnel, and general culture that improve governmental performance overall and are not restricted to the particular practice at hand. They are also likely to vary somewhat between the settings where the practice can be successfully implemented.

To take a further illustration, consider the high-expectations welfare-to-work program. The definitional essence has to do with creating a certain kind of psychological environment for the participants in the program. The administrative features having to do with recruitment, training, supervision, and so on are important supportive features, and almost certainly worth analyzing in any account of how to make such a program work, but we should not characterize them as an "essential" element of the "practice."

One of the two most deadly pitfalls of smart practice analysis is misconstruing which elements of a practice are doing the basic causal work, either alone or in combination. (The other one is wrongly believing that the practice is what is responsible for whatever good—or bad—results have been observed.) A full discussion of this issue is beyond our scope.[10] Suffice it to say here that analysis of the basic causal structure must focus on how the practice takes advantage of some latent opportunity for creating value on the cheap. Furthermore, the analysis should make use of whatever empirical comparisons and contrasts can help sharpen the causal picture (e.g., among instances of the practice as implemented in different contexts but with varying degrees of success).

Distinguish between "essential" and "optional" elements. Optional elements I define as those that add some dimension of value to the outcome that not every user of the practice might want, whereas essential elements are those that every user would want. In the milestones case, the element that, in Oklahoma, had clients sitting down with the contractor and discussing whether particular milestones had been met seems to me to merit being treated as optional. Not every user of the milestones practice would value the relationship-building contribution of this element.

---

10. Interpretation of the "essential" causal elements of a smart practice, or what does the "basic causal work," is a deeply theoretical act. Theoretical perspectives, of course, differ widely among social scientists, among policy analysts, and among ordinary people who would never think of themselves as being "theoretical" at all. An account of my own theoretical perspective, which is based on the metaphor of *craftsmanship*, may be found in my *Getting Agencies to Work Together: The Practice and Theory of Managerial Craftsmanship* (Washington, D.C.: Brookings Institution, 1998), particularly chaps. 2 and 9.

Distinguish between the functions each of the elements performs and the methods used to perform them. Note that in my characterization of milestone payments to contractors I spoke of elements such as defining milestones and verifying claims of achievement—functions to be performed—but left the methods unspecified. And in characterizing the essence of the high-expectations welfare-to-work program I referred to "creating a certain kind of psychological environment" without specifying the methods. It is generally desirable to use this functional characterization of the elements that go to make up a practice and thus to leave open to local option exactly how to carry the functions out. In other words, the functional characterization works as a statement at an abstract level of an end or result to be achieved by some component within a functioning system, and it avoids tying the definition of the practice to exactly what that component must look like. A linguistic hint: To characterize functions, use gerunds—that is, verblike nouns ending in *ing*—as I did above with *defining, verifying,* and *creating.*

The exceptions to the principle of relying on functional language arise when you really need or want to specify a particular method for carrying out a function. In the milestones case I intentionally referred to a contract as a specific means of defining expectations among the parties and to documents as a means of attesting that the milestones had been met.

Allowing for Variation and Complexity

Characterization should be generic and flexible, not prescriptive and overly precise. Consider the expenditure control budget described earlier. Is the "practice" there giving *all* the savings back to the department, or would, say, 50 percent qualify? If the idea is to provide incentives to spend wisely, probably 50 percent would do. Probably the best characterization would be "allowing the department to retain *enough* of the savings for them to feel motivated to create the savings in the first place."[11] It would be left up to whoever implements the expenditure control budget to determine what *enough* means in the local context.

I would also say that it *should* be left to local implementers to figure out the details of the generic practice that make sense in their own context. Allowing for local adaptation of nonessential elements not only serves common sense but also encourages greater buy-in by locals of a practice that in some sense is being imported from elsewhere or, worse yet, imposed from outside.

---

11. Note that this is an interpretation asserted by the researcher-observer, not necessarily something that has actually been done in practice or endorsed by any practitioners.

Characterization of the essential elements of a practice is not necessarily simple; it could be complex. In my list of examples of candidate smart practices, I included only relatively simple practices, so as not to cause confusion. However, some smart practices are multifaceted, complex, and not easy to summarize in a few sentences or even paragraphs. Michael Barzelay analyzed what he called the "postbureaucratic paradigm" for managing statewide overhead and control functions in Minnesota state government. He considered trying to reduce the many aspects of this postbureaucratic paradigm—which I would also call a smart practice, albeit a very large practice—to a few "core ideas" such as "service," "customer focus," "quality," "incentives," "creating value," and "empowerment." But, he concluded, "the major concepts . . . are not organized hierarchically, with one master idea at the top." Instead, we are working with "an extended family of ideas."[12]

A related management reform paradigm, called by many the *new public management* (NPM), emerged in New Zealand in the mid-1980s and is also an "extended family" of ideas and practices. One observer notes that it "is not reducible to a few sentences, let alone a slogan" and goes on to state its "key ideas":

- Government should provide high-quality services that citizens value;
- The autonomy of public managers, particularly from central agency controls, should be increased;
- Organizations and individuals should be evaluated and rewarded on the basis of how well they meet demanding performance targets;
- Managers must be assured that the human and technological resources they need to perform well will be available to them;
- Public sector managers must appreciate the value of competition and maintain an open-minded attitude about which services belong in the private, rather than public, sector.[13]

Specimens of a smart practice in the real world look rather different from one another and require careful interpretation. You should try to find multiple exemplars or specimens of a smart practice to get a sense of its robustness and efficacy when (1) it is being implemented under different supportive (or antagonistic) conditions, (2) it comes with different optional features attached, and (3) it employs supposedly equivalent but nevertheless somewhat different means to perform the required functions. Ideally, you would be able to find social

---

12. Michael Barzelay, *Breaking through Bureaucracy: A New Vision for Managing in Government* (Berkeley: University of California Press, 1992), 115–17.
13. Borins, *Innovating with Integrity*, 9.

scientific evaluation studies of practices that would supply both data and theoretical interpretation regarding such matters. In most cases, however, such evaluations will not exist. Normally—or perhaps at best—you will finds writings or speeches by practitioners describing successes in a few places, accompanied by only sketchy descriptions of what was done or the difficulties of implementation. You will need to think very hard and reason very carefully about how you will want to conceptualize (that is, define) the smart practice of interest and to assess the support requirements you think are the most important. You need to do this even before you get to thinking about how the practice might work in the particular context(s) you have in mind—see the discussion headed "But Will It Work Here?"

Generic Vulnerabilities

It should be part of standard professional practice in describing smart practices to explain not only how and why they work but also how and why they fail, collapse, backfire, and generally make people sorry they ever tried them. That is, we should be told the nature of their *generic vulnerabilities*. A generic vulnerability is a potential weakness of the practice that is somehow connected with its basic causal structure. It might have to do with a high sensitivity to small errors in execution. Or it might have to do with the environment in which the practice is being implemented (e.g., an environment that might impose certain insupportable stresses).

Of course, all political and implementation environments are stressful to a certain degree, and we can reasonably include in the "essential" definition of a particular smart practice those features necessary to safeguard it against the more predictable and potentially damaging stresses. Without such safeguards an otherwise smart practice could become a very dumb practice! For instance, if privatizing certain municipal service functions is a smart practice when would-be private suppliers operate in a competitive market, it might become a very dumb practice: if it were to be carried out in an environment monopolized by a single supplier; if the bidding process is very corruptible and corrupt interests were to discover this fact; if inappropriate performance measures were to be stipulated in the contract; or if the municipal contract management procedures were overly rigid or overly lax. To take another example, a high-expectations welfare-to-work program is vulnerable to the condition of the local labor market. If unemployment is high and jobs are scarce, high expectations will produce in participants more defeatism about themselves and more cynicism about the "responsibility" that society is urging on them. A government-neighborhood "partnership" regarding parks is, in a generic sense, vulnerable to, among other things, temptations on the part of policymakers to slowly shift more and more burdens onto neighbors while reallocating budgetary funds to other departments.

Generic vulnerabilities are only the *potential* for trouble, it should be remembered. Whether the troubles actually materialize depends on the nature of the local environment in which the smart practice is implemented and on the success of various parties who are aware of the vulnerabilities in designing and implementing successful countermeasures. Contracting processes, for instance, can be designed to minimize corruption, albeit at some cost. And neighbors entering into a partnership with the city regarding parks maintenance might insist on putting the terms of the partnership in writing and holding a well-photographed press conference to announce them. Even if such a document had no legal standing, it would give neighborhood representatives in later years some useful political leverage.

Two particular types of vulnerability are especially worth attending to. One pertains to likely failures of general management capacity (e.g., a low general level of leadership talent or the lack of a "good government" ethos that would make it easier to implement this or any other practice successfully). The other pertains to weaknesses intrinsic to the particular practice itself (e.g., a susceptibility to conflict in some service delivery program over whether to give priority to this or that catchment area or needy subpopulation or, in some safety-oriented regulatory program, whether to err on the side of injury-tolerant leniency or costly stringency).

But Will It Work Here?

Assuming that you have understood the essence of the generic smart practice very well, including its generic vulnerabilities, and have mapped the variety of supportive elements that could increase its odds of success, in the end, you must still ask: Assuming this practice is indeed smart in some contexts, is ours a context in which it can work well enough to warrant trying it? Answering this question intelligently entails looking at both the source contexts, where the practice appears to have worked well, and at your own target context, where it is being considered for adoption.

The Target Context

Within your target context, a careful assessment of the present situation is in order, of course, but a static answer based on this assessment is not enough. You need to think also about what might be done at reasonable cost or risk to improve the prospects of the smart practice in the target context were it to be implemented there. These actions fall into two categories: possible safeguarding strategies and possible enhancement strategies.

First, consider safeguarding strategies. These have to do with the generic vulnerabilities of the smart practice. Are the most dangerous of them likely to cause unacceptable trouble in your context? For instance, if excessive rigidity in the contract management process is a generic vulnerability of partnering with a nonprofit agency, are your contract management institutions known to be unusually rigid? And if so, is there anything you can do to offset this problem? Might you, for instance, find someone in the contract management bureau who can serve as a special protector and expediter? Or if you cannot do that, can you find some way to structure the contract terms so that the contractor is held accountable for achieving general results rather than for following specific procedures?

Regarding enhancement strategies, consider what I have called above the *supportive elements* that can help a practice work relatively better. What supportive elements will be put into play? How well are they likely to perform? Can you do anything to improve them? For instance, can you attract top-notch personnel to manage this program or undertake this project? Can you obtain more stable funding than annual appropriations? Can you mobilize the press to take positive notice of what you are doing? Can you count on the support of key stakeholders and relevant political constituencies—or at least on weak action from opponents?

The Source Contexts

If you have to search very hard for smart practices that might be usable in your own situation, the chances are that the practice will not be very widespread. This means that the specimens you locate will come from jurisdictions, agencies, or locales where policymakers and administrators tend to look more favorably on novelty and innovation than is usually the case. Hence, their overall managerial capacity may be better than average, and perhaps better than the one in your own locale.

If the source contexts are largely pilot or demonstration programs, you need to be particularly cautious, because

- Pilot program implementers probably bring more enthusiasm and talent to bear on their work than the average program implementers, and enthusiasm and talent count for something.
- The political and financial conditions at the pilot sites are probably more favorable (or less unfavorable) than those at the average site.

- Bureaucratic resistance to a pilot is typically less intense than to a permanent change that threatens existing values, status, job security, or work routines.

How cautious should you be in extrapolating from successes observed in pilot or demonstration contexts? No systematic research exists to answer this question. However, a RAND Corporation analysis of a variety of juvenile crime prevention programs discounted the effectiveness levels attained in the pilot contexts by 15 to 40 percent when estimating a "scaling up penalty" that would apply when implementing the programs on a wide scale.[14] Although the RAND analysts offered no explicit reasoning for choosing the penalty factors that they did, their choices do seem reasonable.

If you are analyzing the possibility of implementing a smart practice not just in some known local context but on a wide scale, you should be concerned about more than the fact that pilot program results may be much better than average. You should also be concerned about the existence of many *below-average* sites where the smart practice would be implemented, some of them perhaps quite a bit below average. In an era when it was much less natural to think about the federal devolution of program and policy responsibilities to state governments than it is today, federal policymakers, particularly political liberals, often worried about the "Mississippi problem." Mississippi was the rhetorical symbol of the poor, backward, and probably racist jurisdiction that would almost surely wreck or pervert any smart practice it was given responsibility for implementing.

Back to the Eightfold Path

Given the typical shortfall of good evidence relative to theory and speculation when it comes to assessing a smart practice, there is a danger of unwarranted optimism. No wonder a common criticism of the best practice research tradition is that it becomes excessively enthusiastic about what appear to be good ideas before their worth is sufficiently tested.[15]

But how much testing is "sufficient," anyway? The answer has to be framed partly in terms of the costs of displacing what might actually be a better practice, perhaps even the practices currently in use (called above, "letting present trends continue"). However, if one is reasonably confident that current practices are

---

14. Peter H. Greenwood, Karyn E. Model, C. Peter Rydell, and James Chiesa, *Diverting Children from a Life of Crime: Measuring Costs and Benefits* (Santa Monica, Calif.: RAND Corporation, 1995).
15. Unfortunately, excessive enthusiasm for experiments that eventually fail gives even appropriate enthusiasm for experimentation a bad name.

ineffective and/or harmful, the costs of wrongly abandoning them in favor of the new and untried may not be so high after all. Thus, although the new and untried should bear *some* burden of proof, it should not be an excessive one. The correct approach is to treat the risks and uncertainties involved in adopting some seemingly smart practice as being on a par with the uncertainties associated with all the other alternatives under consideration.

Of course, the costs of change—negotiation, insecurity, hard feelings, and so on—must also be counted against bringing in a new and seemingly smart practice. But such costs must be counted against any change, not just change to accommodate smart practice. Moreover, if institutions and people are very stuck in their ways, there may be benefits to change as such, not merely costs.[16]

---

16. Alternatively, if institutions and people are forever being reformed and reinvented and remodeled—as occurs in many public school systems—there may be benefits to stability, consistency, and focus.

Things Governments Do

THE FOLLOWING LIST of "things governments do" is meant to stimulate creativity and give you ideas. The way to use it is to think about your policy problem and then go down the list, asking yourself, "Might there be any way to use this approach on this problem?"

The "why you might do it" discussion that accompanies each list of "what you might do" is necessarily brief. It is intended principally to be suggestive.

I. Taxes

A. What You Might Do

1. Add a new tax
2. Abolish an old tax
3. Change tax rate
4. Change tax base
5. Improve collection machinery
6. Tax an externality

B. Why You Might Do It

The most common conditions in which taxes are a solution are when there is inadequate government revenue for some purpose and—probably more important—when the structure of market prices fails to capture the true economic opportunity costs. If market prices are wrong, there are usually deeper structural reasons, like oligopolistic power or government overregulation of some input, which might bear correcting by other means as well.

Naturally, too many taxes can also be a problem. They may be inhibiting useful economic or social activity.

II. Regulation

A. What You Might Do

1. Add a new regulatory regime or abolish an old one
2. Write new standards or remove old ones
3. Tighten or loosen existing standards
4. Improve scientific and technical basis for writing standards
5. Close or open loopholes
6. Add, train, or better supervise enforcement personnel
7. Improve targeting of enforcement to catch bad apples, or to increase deterrence, or to increase resource efficiency
8. Raise or lower level of effective sanctions
9. Tighten or loosen appeals procedures
10. Change reporting and auditing procedures
11. Add, subtract, or improve complaint mechanisms for workers or public

B. Why You Might Do It

Distinguish three quite different types of regulation. One aims at prices and outputs in natural monopolies. The public utilities commission regulating local telephone service is an example.

A second type—sometimes called *social regulation*—is common in regard to health and safety issues. It aims to correct imperfections arising from poor market information or from excessive frictions resulting from the use of civil law (usually, tort or contract) remedies. Drug safety regulation by the FDA is an example. In this type of regulation, two sorts of problems are common: too little and too much. Scientific uncertainties, technical difficulties of measurement, and political pressures typically lead to both of these problems under varying conditions.

A third type of regulation concerns entry, exit, output, price, and service levels in supposedly oligopolistic industries (e.g., transportation). Administering this type of regulation presents large problems of information collection and of coordinating the outputs of many firms. Politically there are often problems of anticompetitive "capture." The deregulation movement since around 1978 has led to a new appreciation of how much beneficial competition there might be in these industries if government were simply to let go.

Most air and water pollution regulation is thought of as social regulation. However, administratively (and sometimes politically) it is more like the third type of regulation, inasmuch as the principal laws now on the books involve government agencies in coordinating the outputs of a variety of firms.

III. Subsidies and Grants

A. What You Might Do

1. Add a new one
2. Abolish an old one
3. Change the level
4. Change the marginal rate
5. Introduce, abolish, or change a formula by which subsidies are allocated
6. Modify the conditions of receipt or eligibility
7. Loosen enforcement
8. Tighten enforcement

B. Why You Might Do It

Incentive effects. Subsidies and grants are often used to stimulate activities that neither markets nor nonprofit nor voluntary action appears to produce in adequate quantity or quality. They also play an important role in the system of intergovernmental relationships, when one level of government wishes to encourage another level of government to do certain things. They also play a role in the system of relationships between governments and nonprofit organizations.

Wealth effects. Grants and subsidies also transfer resources to people or organizations or levels of government in order to make the recipients wealthier.

Some design problems. It often happens that you want to create incentive effects but not wealth effects, or vice versa. For instance, you might wish to make poor people wealthier via grants and subsidies but without diminishing work incentives. Or you might wish to encourage businesses or universities to undertake more research and development of a certain kind but without unduly enriching them or allowing them to use the subsidies inefficiently.

Note that subsidies and grants are typically administered with various guidelines or conditions attached. The threat to remove a long-time grant or subsidy for violation of the guidelines or conditions can act as a type of regulatory sanction, therefore, making certain grants and subsidies into a peculiar regulatory hybrid.

IV. Provide a Service

A. What You Might Do

1. Add a new service
2. Expand an existing service
3. Organize outreach to potential beneficiaries not now using the service
4. Better customize an existing service to a particular subpopulation.
5. Provide people with vouchers for a particular service so they may choose from an array of competitive service providers
6. Link two or more existing service delivery systems to take advantage of potential synergies or to make life easier for service recipients
7. Reduce the difficulties for service users of accessing the service by
   a. Going on line
   b. Computerizing intake and eligibility processes
   c. Simplifying forms
   d. Colocating services
   e. Permitting appointments by phone
   f. Facilitating personal inquiries and complaints
   g. Improving payment options

B. Why You Might Do It

Services come in two basic flavors. Desired services are those people want, like parks and good schools. Paternalistic services are those that people might or might not desire but that outsiders want them to have because there is some potential payoff to the outsiders (e.g., rehabilitative services for the mentally ill, organized shelters for the homeless, job search services for individuals on welfare). It is a lot easier to design a service provision system for desired services than to do so for paternalistic services.

V. Agency Budgets

A. What You Might Do

1. Add a lot to the budget
2. Add just a little to the budget
3. Hold the budget at last year's level
4. Cut the budget a little

5. Cut the budget a lot—to the point of beginning to terminate the agency
6. Shift allocations from one budget item to another

B. Why You Might Do It

You might want to adjust an agency's budget according to whether you like what it does. In addition, how you manipulate an agency's budget sends political signals about the degree of satisfaction or dissatisfaction with the agency's performance and so may be thought to have incentive effects as well as wealth effects. It is not easy to use the budget as a means of creating incentive effects, however.

VI. Information

A. What You Might Do

1. Require disclosure
2. Direct government rating or certification
3. Standardize display or format
4. Simplify information
5. Subsidize production of information
6. Subsidize dissemination of information

B. Why You Might Do It

Information production, dissemination, and validation may be suboptimal due to the declining average (and sometimes marginal) cost nature of the activity. Information consumption may be suboptimal due to the hidden costs of consumption (such as time spent reading or hearing or interpreting or sifting or verifying).

VII. Modify Structure of Private Rights

A. What You Might Modify or Create

1. Contract rights and duties
2. Property rights
3. Liability duties
4. Family law

5. Constitutional rights
6. Labor law
7. Corporate law
8. Criminal law
9. Dispute-resolving institutions other than litigation and courts

B. Why You Might Do It

In recent years, two of the biggest issues that have attracted the attention of policy analysts and economists interested in legal institutions concern the economically efficient incidence of risk—it should fall on the party that can manage it at the lowest social cost—and the costs involved in administering any adjudicative system. Since private-law duties and rights do a lot to allocate risk (e.g., if your product exposes the user to risk and ultimately injury, you may be liable for damages, unless perhaps the user abused or misused it or agreed to assume the risks of use), adjusting laws is sometimes a powerful policy intervention mechanism. As to the administrative and adjudicative costs, much creative thinking has gone into finding ways to bring these down.

In addition to these economic concerns, there is also concern about compensation for harms. Laws can be changed so as to shift wealth—in some prospectively actuarial sense or in a real present-time sense—among different interests or classes of people.

The wealth-shifting and risk-shifting effects of legal changes may both work in the desired direction, or they may work at cross-purposes. In addition both may work together with, or at cross-purposes with, the desire to reduce administrative and adjudicative costs.

VIII. Modify Framework of Economic Activity

A. What You Might Do

1. Encourage competition
2. Encourage concentration
3. Control prices and wages (and profits)
4. Decontrol prices and wages (and profits)
5. Control output levels
6. Decontrol output levels

7. Change tax incentives up or down
8. Provide public jobs
9. Abolish public jobs

B. Why You Might Do It

Supporting more government intervention. On the supply side, there may be monopoly or oligopoly problems. On the demand side, consumers may be relatively nonmobile or otherwise vulnerable to exploitation—and the same might be true of workers.

Supporting less government intervention. You might decide that political forces have captured the government administrative apparatus and perverted the intent, or you might decide that the information costs to government entailed in doing the job well are simply too high, or you might think that technology has changed and made an older form of government intervention less appropriate or effective or efficient.

IX. Education and Consultation

A. What You Might Do

1. Warn of hazards or dangers
2. Raise consciousness through exhortation or inspiration
3. Provide technical assistance
4. Upgrade skills and competencies
5. Change values
6. Professionalize the providers of a service through training or certification or licensing

B. Why You Might Do It

People may be unaware of a problem or an opportunity. They may be careless or unfeeling. There might be too many untrained or unskilled people in jobs demanding too much responsibility.

X. Financing and Contracting

A. What You Might Do

1. Create a new (governmental) market
2. Abolish an existing (governmental) market
3. Alter reimbursement rates
4. Change the basis for reimbursement (e.g., cost-plus, price per unit, sliding scale dependent on quantity, performance bonuses or penalties)
5. Lease governmentally held resources
6. Alter user fee structure
7. Redesign bidding systems
8. Change contract enforcement methods
9. Furnish loans
10. Guarantee loans
11. Subsidize loans
12. Set up a public enterprise
13. Dismantle a public enterprise
14. "Privatize" a hitherto public enterprise
15. Modify insurance arrangements
16. Change procurement practices

B. Why You Might Do It

Capital and/or insurance markets might be working inefficiently. The governmental contracting and procurement machinery might not be operating well: it might be too rigid, or too corrupt, or too expensive, or too slow.

XI. Bureaucratic and Political Reforms

A. What You Might Do

The number of possibilities is too great to list. It ranges across such activities as reorganizations, replacing top supervisory personnel, improving information systems, and raising wages and salaries.

B. Why You Might Do It

The substantive reasons are too numerous to list. We may note, though, that in many policy contexts there are important political and symbolic considerations for undertaking bureaucratic and political reforms. The political considerations often involve enhancing the power of one social interest or point of view at the expense of another. The symbolic considerations often involve ducking the really hard or impossible problems at the social level in favor of doing something readily seen in a domain over which government appears to have control (that is, its own operations).

Semantic Tips: A Summary

AN UNUSUAL CONTRIBUTION of this book is the number of semantic tips it contains, tips for using language to make the work of the analyst easier and to avoid pitfalls. It is surprising how easily the right small words can improve understanding and the wrong ones can mire us in confusion. In this appendix I collect the principal semantic tips to be found throughout the text. I edit the text slightly in some cases.

Defining the Problem

- It often—but not always—helps to think in terms of deficit and excess, for instance, "There are too many homeless people in the United States." To focus on deficit and excess, it often helps to include the word *too* in the problem definition: "too big," "too small," "growing too slowly," "growing too fast." These last two phrases (about growing) remind us that problems deserving our attention don't necessarily exist today but are (at least potentially) in prospect for the future, whether near or distant.

- Most good problem definitions are limited to *description*. Problem definitions that explicitly or implicitly also include a *diagnosis of the causes* of some problem can be treacherous. Consider, for instance, "In the air pollution area, the problem is that states have not been willing to force motorists to keep their engines tuned up and their exhaust systems in proper order." Suppose, though, that the causal diagnosis is mistaken or misleading (e.g., that states' unwillingness to enforce engine maintenance routines is *not* in fact a very important cause of air pollution). Because *definition* in some contexts connotes legitimate arbitrariness ("I'll define *justice* to mean . . ."), the causal claims implicit in diagnostic problem definitions can easily escape needed scrutiny.

- Your problem definition should not include an implicit solution introduced by semantic carelessness. Projected solutions must be evaluated empirically and not legitimated merely by definition. Therefore, keep the
  problem definition stripped down to a mere description, and leave open
  where you will look for solutions. Don't say, "There is too little shelter
  for homeless families." This formulation might inadvertently imply that
  "more shelter" is the best solution and might inhibit you from thinking
  about ways to prevent families from becoming homeless in the first place.
  Try instead, "There are too many homeless families."
- A tip-off that you're probably smuggling an implicit solution into the
  problem definition is to hear yourself saying, "Aha, but that's not the
  real problem; the real problem is . . ." While there are better and worse
  ways to conceptualize a problem, or to solve a problem, it stretches ordinary usage too much to say that one problem could be "more (less) real"
  than another.

Assembling the Evidence

Data are facts—or some might say, representations of facts—about the world.
Data include all sorts of statistics but go well beyond statistics, too. Data also
include, for instance, facts about an agency manager's ability to deal constructively
with the press. *Information* is data that have meaning, in the sense that they can
help you sort the world into different logical or empirical categories. The prevalence
of cigarette smoking in five different countries is "data," but these data become
"information" when you decide it is interesting to array the countries comparatively
(e.g., from lowest to highest prevalence). *Evidence* is information that affects the
existing beliefs of important people (including yourself) about significant features
of the problem you are studying and how it might be solved or mitigated.
Differential prevalence of smoking, for instance, can become evidence bearing
on hypotheses about different levels of concern about personal health across
countries.

Constructing the Alternatives

- Always include in your first approach to the problem the alternative "Let
  present trends continue undisturbed." You need to do this because the
  world is full of naturally occurring changes, and some of these ongoing
  changes might mitigate the problem on which you are working. (Note
  that I am not characterizing this alternative as "Do nothing." It is not

possible to "do nothing." Most of the trends in motion will probably persist and alter the problem, whether for better or for worse.)

- The key to simplifying your menu of alternatives, which can become lengthy and complex, is to distinguish between a basic alternative and its variants. The basic element in many policy alternatives is an intervention strategy, such as regulatory enforcement or a subsidy or a tax incentive, that causes people or institutions to change their conduct in some way. But no intervention strategy can stand alone; it must be implemented by some agency or constellation of agencies (perhaps including nonprofit organizations), and it must have a source of financing. Usually the variants on the basic strategy are defined by different methods of implementation and different methods of financing.

- *Alternative* does not necessarily signify that the policy options are mutually exclusive. Among policy analysts the term *alternative* is used ambiguously. Sometimes it means that choosing one implies forgoing another, and sometimes it means simply one more policy action that might help solve or mitigate some problem, perhaps in conjunction with other alternatives. Sometimes you won't be entirely sure whether two alternatives are or are not mutually exclusive. For instance, the mayor earlier might have promised enough money to either fix potholes or provide homeless shelters (but not both), but you may have made such a great case for both programs that the mayor might decide to increase the budgetary allocation.

Selecting Criteria

- Evaluative criteria are *not* used to judge the alternatives, or at least not directly. They are to be applied to the projected outcomes. It is easy to get confused about this point. This confusion is encouraged by a common-sense way of speaking: "Alternative A looks to be the best—therefore let's proceed with it." But this way of speaking ignores a very important step. The complete formulation is "Alternative A will very probably lead to Outcome O_A, which we judge to be the best of the possible outcomes; therefore, we judge Alternative A to be the best." Applying criteria to the evaluation of outcomes and not alternatives makes it possible to remember that we might like O_A a great deal even if, because we lacked sufficient confidence that A would actually lead to O_A, we decided not to choose Alternative A after all. With that judgment on the table, it would be possible to look for other alternatives with a greater likelihood of producing O_A.

- If it is possible to sort your criteria into those that refer to values to be maximized, values that stand as constraints, and values that have a more-is-better quality, keep the different statuses of the criteria in mind. Be conscious of them. You can do this with a simple verbal trick: As appropriate, define your criteria as "Maximize such-and-such value"; "Satisfy such-and-such value constraint"; and "Get more of such-and-such value."

Projecting Outcomes

- Assuming for the moment that benefits are uncertain while costs are not, ask yourself these two questions: (1) "Given what I know for sure about the costs of this alternative, what is the minimum help we need to get from Condition X to ensure adequately offsetting benefits?" and (2) "How reasonable is it to believe that Condition X will actually produce that minimum?" Question 1 can also be framed in terms of known benefits and the conditions that would yield minimally acceptable costs.
- Implementation scenarios should be written in the future perfect tense. This encourages concreteness, which is a helpful stimulant to the imagination.
- Analysts are often cautioned to think about *unanticipated consequences.* But this term is not appropriate, for it is often used to refer to perfectly anticipatable, though undesirable, side effects. Here are some common undesirable but anticipatable side effects in public programs:
- A common error that occurs in labeling the "criterion" columns in an outcomes matrix is to fail to indicate what *value* is at stake and in what dimensions the measurement is being done. For instance, if you are assessing a rental subsidy program, and you enter a + in a column labeled "Landlord/tenant relations," the reader may not know whether you think relations will become more harmonious, more confrontational, less dominated by landlords, less dominated by tenants, or something else. It is not sufficient that your surrounding text makes your intention clear; the matrix labeling itself must be informative. In my illustrative matrix I did not simply write "Cleanup" or "Cost" or "Time." Within the space constraints I tried to indicate the metric and the desired direction it should move in. In many cases it helps to insert *maximize* or *minimize* in the criterion label.

Confronting Trade-offs

- As economics teaches us, trade-offs occur at the margin. Trade-off analysis tells us something like this: "If we spend an extra X dollars for an extra unit of Service Y, we can get an extra Z units of good outcome." This puts the decision maker in the position to answer the question: Does society (or do you) value Z more or less than X? and then to follow the obvious implication of the answer (if yes, decide for another Y; if no, don't). A linguistic device to help you keep focused on the margin is frequent use of the word *extra*. Note that this word appears three times in the sentence quoted in this paragraph.
- A common pitfall in confronting trade-offs is to think and speak of the tradeoffs as being across *alternatives* rather than across projected *outcomes* (e.g., "trading off twenty foot patrol officers in the late night hours against a lower-maintenance-cost fleet of police vehicles." Although there is such a trade-off, you'll see, with a second's thought, that you can't do anything at all with it. Both alternatives must first be converted into outcomes before genuine trade-offs can be confronted. Thus, the competing outcomes might be fifty (plus or minus) burglaries per year prevented by the patrol officers versus a savings of $300,000 in fleet maintenance.
- To simplify comparisons and help you focus on key trade-offs, set up benchmarks with one or more "base cases." The most commonly used base case is the set of outcomes you associate with the alternative "letting present trends continue." Other possibly illuminating base cases are:

"The likely outcome if we don't manage to head off what the Governor's office [or some other powerful faction] is planning . . ."

"Our ideal set of outcomes if political [or other] conditions were just a bit more favorable . . ."

"Our ideal set of outcomes if we were to weight [some particular] criterion as heavily as we think we ought to . . ."

"The worst-case scenario which we have to prevent practically at any cost . . ."

Doing Smart Practices Research

- Don't be misled by the *best* in best practices research. Rarely will you have any confidence that some helpful-looking practice is actually the "best" among all those that are addressed to the same problem or opportunity. The extensive and careful research to document a claim of best will almost never have been done. Usually you will be looking for what, more modestly, might be called good practices.

- I have made a point, in describing each of the supposedly smart practices, of saying that the practice "takes advantage" of something. This is a linguistic device for ensuring that in analyzing how the practice works, we make sure to focus on those aspects of its works that are central, that is, on the fact that the practice aims to exploit, to take advantage of, some latent opportunity for creating value on the cheap.

- Distinguish between elements of a practice that are essential and those that are supportive. The essential elements are also the ones that do the basic causal work of the practice, that is, produce the valued results of the practice. These elements are essential in both a definitional and a causal sense.

- In characterizing the elements of a practice, distinguish between the functions that each of the elements performs and the methods used to perform them. Note that in Part III on smart practices, in my characterization of milestone payments to contractors, I spoke of elements like defining milestones and verifying claims of achievement—functions to be performed—but left the methods unspecified. And in characterizing the essence of the high-expectations welfare-to-work program, I referred to "creating a certain kind of psychological environment" without specifying the methods. It is generally desirable to use this functional characterization of the elements that go to make up a practice and thus to leave open to local option exactly how to carry the functions out. In other words, the functional characterization works as a statement at an abstract level of an end or result to be achieved by some component within a functioning system, and it avoids tying the definition of the practice to exactly what that component must look like. A linguistic hint: To characterize functions, use gerunds—that is, verblike nouns ending in *ing*—as I did above with *defining, verifying,* and *creating.*